Strategic Marketing

■ ■ ■

SCHOOL LEADERSHIP AND MANAGEMENT SERIES

Series Editors: Brent Davies and John West-Burnham

Other titles in the series:

Effective Learning in Schools
by Christopher Bowring-Carr and John West-Burnham

Middle Management in Schools
by Sonia Blandford

Reengineering and Total Quality in Schools
by Brent Davies and John West-Burnham

Forthcoming titles:

Human Resource Management for Effective Schools
by John O'Neill and John West-Burnham

Management Development
by John West-Burnham

Managing Quality in Schools
by John West-Burnham

Resource Management in Schools
by Sonia Blandford

Strategic Development Planning for Schools
by Brent Davies and Linda Ellison

Strategic Marketing for Schools

■ ■ ■

How to Harmonise Marketing and Strategic Development for an Effective School

BRENT DAVIES AND
LINDA ELLISON

FINANCIAL TIMES
PITMAN PUBLISHING

This book is dedicated to Cassandra Brent Davies for gaining a place at Sidney Sussex College, Cambridge

FINANCIAL TIMES
MANAGEMENT

LONDON · SAN FRANCISCO
KUALA LUMPUR · JOHANNESBURG

Financial Times Management delivers the knowledge, skills and understanding that enable students, managers and organisations to achieve their ambitions, whatever their needs, wherever they are.

London Office:
128 Long Acre, London WC2E 9AN
Tel: +44 (0)171 447 2000
Fax: +44 (0)171 240 5771
Website: www.ftmanagement.com

A Division of Financial Times Professional Limited

First published in Great Britain in 1997

ISBN 0 273 62408 3

British Library Cataloguing in Publication Data
A CIP catalogue record for this book can be obtained from the British Library

10 9 8 7 6 5 4 3 2

Typeset by Phoenix Photosetting, Chatham, Kent
Printed and bound in Great Britain by Redwood Books, Trowbridge, Wiltshire.

The Publishers' policy is to use paper manufactured from sustainable forests.

Contents

■ ■ ■

Preface *vii*

Acknowledgements *viii*

Part One
THE NATURE AND DIMENSIONS OF MARKETING 1

1 Marketing and Markets *3*

2 The Process of Marketing *16*

Part Two
STRATEGIC INTENT 27

3 Creating Strategic Intent *29*

Part Three
STRATEGIC MARKET ANALYSIS 39

4 The Market Research Process *41*

5 Analysing the Environment *50*

6 Analysing the Competitors *57*

7 Analysing the Clients *76*

8 Analysing the School *99*

9 Integrating and Interpreting the Marketing Evidence *118*

Part Four
MARKETING IMPLEMENTATION 141

10 Marketing Techniques and Approaches *143*

11 Implementing the Marketing Plan *181*

12 Evaluating the Marketing Process *193*

Appendix 1 Categorised questions *199*

Appendix 2 Randomised questionnaires *209*

Appendix 3 Investigating the attitudes of Years 1 and 2 at Buswells Lodge Primary School *223*

Index *228*

Preface

■ ■ ■

When we wrote our first book on marketing in 1991 it was one of a number of attempts to apply the traditional business approaches of marketing to the education sector. One of our key concepts in that early book was that 'marketing was a process, not an event'. Our research in schools had shown that as a result of the competitive pressures resulting from the 1988 Education Reform Act schools had engaged in a series of marketing responses. What was clear, however, was that these responses were often not part of an integrated marketing process but were a series of isolated events. Our book addressed that problem.

Researching and working as consultants with senior management teams in schools over the ensuing six years has further extended and deepened our work. The results of this extended research and experience have increased our understanding of the importance of the strategic dimensions of marketing. Thus we have engaged in a major reconstruction and reinterpretation of our earlier work to produce this current volume. This book is organised in four parts. The nature and dimensions of marketing are considered in Part One, while Part Two highlights the significance of creating strategic intent in the staff of the school. Part Three describes the series of stages involved in building up a strategic market analysis from which to create a marketing plan. In Part Four, we consider marketing techniques and approaches, the implementation of the plan and the evaluation of the effectiveness of the marketing process.

As schools move towards the challenge of providing effective education for the new millennium, one of the key tasks will be enhancing the capacity of their staff to lead and manage in this increasingly complex environment. In our leadership development work we often talk about developing leadership in depth in a school and developing strategic capacity in those leaders. The role of a headteacher in this context is to be a leader of educational leaders, with leadership dispersed throughout the organisation. To that end we see the significance of this book as one which takes our definition of marketing in education as *the means by which the school actively communicates and promotes its purpose, values and products to the pupils, parents, staff and wider community* and makes it the wider responsibility of all those in leadership roles in schools to engage in the strategic marketing process.

We hope you will find this book both valuable and enjoyable.

Brent Davies and Linda Ellison

Acknowledgements

We have been supported in our work by headteachers and deputy headteachers in a number of schools. We acknowledge their contribution here. To any we have omitted, we apologise.

We would like to thank the following individuals who have assisted us in our marketing research projects:

Jane Allen, Salisbury School;
Max Amesbury, Gledhow Primary School;
Linda Bamford, Sir Charles Lucas School and the Mayflower County High School;
Nigel Blackburn, The Hayesbrook School;
Martin Brewis, The Mirfield Free Grammar School;
Geoff Broughton, The Thomas Aveling School;
Carol Buchanan, St Augustine's Catholic GM School;
Tony Buckley, George Tomlinson (GM) School;
Steve Burgoyne, Sexey's School;
David Burrage, Gosbecks Primary School;
Eamonn Cahill, Southlands Community School;
John Cain, Reigate School;
Peter Carrigan, Horndean Community School;
Michael Carter, Highams Park School;
John Catton, Babington Community College;
Malcolm Christian, Oak Farm Community School;
Pat Collarbone, Haggerston School;
William Cosh, Kibble Education and Care Centre;
David Cox, Lincoln Christ's Hospital School;
Terry Creissen, The Colne Community College;
David Crossley, Cirencester Deer Park School;
Janet Cullen-Cornelius, Lea Valley High School;
Roger Evans, Tendring High School;
Steve Fowler, Radyr Comprehensive School;
Valerie Fry, Hamilton County Primary School;
Rod Goldswain, Northampton School for Boys;
Kathleen Griffin, Greenford High School;
Brian Hall, Addingham Middle School;
Peter Hargrave, Broughton Junior School;
Chris Harris, Derham Church First School;
Cheryl Heron, St Edmond's Girls School;
Diana Hiles, Chase Community School;
Andrew Hobbs, Copperfields College;
Caroline Hobbs, The Philip Morant School;
Sarah Jackson, Parayhouse School;
Rachel Jaye, Lee Manor High School and Community College;
Alan Jones, Bexleyheath School;
Susan Jowett, Holly Lodge School, Liverpool;
Michael Kell, Burwood Park School and College;
Mark Lloyd, Barking Abbey School;
Michael Marchant, Howard of Effingham School;
Sally Marshall, Coquet High School;
Bernice McCabe, Chelmsford County High School;
Jean Millham, Morningside Primary School;

George Milne, Peterhead Academy;
Brindley Morgan, Walworth School;
Tony Perrett, Highams Park School;
Michel Riley, Buswells Lodge Primary School;
Chris Roberts, Smithills School;
Lorna Roberts, The Holt School;
Fiona Robinson, Jessons CE Primary School;
David Rowlinson, Sir Frank Markham Community School;
Peter Rubery, Ercall Wood School;
Roger Shortt, Hounslow Manor School;
Nayland Southorn, Sir John Talbot's School;
Roland Sterry, Hodge Hill Girls' School;
Alan Stevens, Sawtry Community College;
Barry Stokes, Colbayns (GM) High School;
Nick Swann, West Somerset Community College;
Jennifer Thomas, Reigate School;
Newton Thompson, New Parks Community College;
Donald Thurlow, St Bede's School;
Vanda Tillotson, The Ashford High School;
Stephen Timbrell, Lakers School;
Eric Tope, St Thomas the Apostle College;
Richard Townsend, Dunraven School;
Tony Tuckwell, King Edward VI Grammar School;
Barbara Vann, Mount Grace High School;
John Versey, Goffs School;
Sister Brenda Wallace, Gumley House School;
Richard Wallis, The Hugh Christie Technology College;
Sue Warrington, Haggerston School;
Virginia Waterhouse, The Leigh City Technology College;
Margaret Wilson, The Helana Romanes School;
Mavis Wilson, Battersea Technology College;
Derek Wise, Cramlington Community High School;
Alison Woodhouse, Warlingham School;
Peter Woods, Haydon School;

In addition we would like to thank:

Mike Billingham;
Broughton Junior School;
The Greenhead Pyramid of schools;
Hounslow Manor School;
The Ilkley Pyramid of schools;
Reigate School;
Surfside Primary School;
Weaver County Primary School.

PART ONE

■ ■ ■

The Nature and Dimensions of Marketing

1 **Marketing and Markets** *3*

2 **The Process of Marketing** *16*

1

■ ■ ■

Marketing and Markets

Virtue does not bring its own reward, but virtue with a good marketing strategy may!

Introduction

There is often confusion between the concepts of *marketing* as a means of communicating specific aspects of an organisation's activities and *markets* as a means of allocating resources. It is important to obtain a clear understanding of this distinction at the outset. In this chapter we will first consider aspects of marketing and the myths and misconceptions that surround it and will then look briefly at educational markets as allocation systems.

What is marketing?

Marketing is about managing relationships through effective communication. In commerce and industry it is often considered to be about managing the exchange between producers and consumers. In the educational world, marketing is about managing the relationship between schools and their clients. We define marketing in education as:

> *the means by which the school actively communicates and promotes its purpose, values and products to the pupils, parents, staff and wider community.* (Davies and Ellison, 1997, p204)

Educationalists are often very suspicious of marketing because of the link with commercialism and selling. The very word seems to sum up high-powered salesmen, plastic packaging, insincerity and something slightly disreputable. Teachers often see marketing as an intrusion on educational values and feel that they should be left to their professional role of teaching children. It is important for schools to realise, however, that they do not exist on an educational desert island, determining what to do and how to do it, but are accountable to the people who fund them and to the communities which they serve. All schools should already be involved in marketing because *every school has a reputation and that reputation has to be managed*.

If marketing is about managing relationships through effective communication, then that communication is, by definition, a two-way process. It is about a transaction between those who provide a product or service and those who receive it. In the context of schools, the outcomes should be agreed and desired both by those providing education and by those receiving it. Therefore marketing in schools is not just about selling the product and service but it is about identifying the nature of what is required by the clients and then ensuring that the school gives ultimate priority to supplying that product and service and to maintaining its quality. If this process is to remain effective, schools must constantly be reviewing their communication strategies.

Why should schools market themselves?

The need to market a school centres around both the communication of the quality of the education offered and the attraction and retention of pupils. Schools often believe that virtue brings its own reward but to be effective, as we move into the twenty-first century, it is not enough simply to be a good school. What is also important is that the school is *perceived* as being a good one. The quote could be rewritten as: Virtue does not bring its own reward, but virtue with a good marketing strategy may! Whatever the positive attributes of a school, they will not, of themselves, ensure continued success and survival unless the wider community knows about, understands and, above all, values them.

One of the prime functions of the marketing process is to ensure two-way communication between the school and its clients. The school must provide information about its aims and achievements to those who have a choice of school and also to the wider group of partners in the educational process, such as industry and the local community. One aspect of this is the collection of information concerning the way in which the external world perceives the school and the expectations which are placed on it. This view is then matched with what the school can offer, so that there is then a coherent information flow on which to base a promotion strategy. These processes are examined in Parts Three and Four of this book.

Much media attention focuses criticism on the education system so there is a significant need to communicate good news in order to provide a balance. Those who work in schools know about the amount of effort that is put in and the excellent achievements of pupils. The marketing process should enable schools to display that quality. While a poor media image serves to lower the morale of teachers and deter entrants to the profession, a positive image will act as a motivating force and should also attract higher quality potential teachers. This not only applies to schools that are struggling to build their reputations but also to those which have already gained good reputations. They still need to manage the marketing process so that the reputation is protected and further enhanced. This is especially the case as other schools begin to raise their profiles in the local community.

The necessity to attract and retain pupils has been brought into sharp focus with the introduction of market forces in the maintained school sector through the 1988 Education Reform Act (DES, 1988). The act enabled the government to continue its policy of reducing the power of monopoly suppliers, in this case the schools and the Local Education Authorities (LEAs), and putting power in the hands of the consumers. This is in line with a number of earlier reforms – for example, the reform of trade union legislation. In education the shift in power can be seen in a variety of ways:

- There has been a very significant reduction in teacher control of the curriculum through the imposition of the national curriculum which has given power to central government.
- Idiosyncratic funding of schools by LEAs has been ended with the development of formula funding.
- The power of school choice has been given to parents through open enrolment.

The two specific aspects of formula funding and open enrolment have a tremendous impact on the need to market a school.

Formula funding has linked pupil numbers and school budgets in a direct way because the more pupils the school has, the more funding it receives. This obviously prioritises the need to attract and retain pupils. However, the effect of formula funding becomes much more dynamic when the impact of open enrolment is taken into account. *Open enrolment* gives the power to parents to send a child to the school of their choice, provided that the school has the physical space to accommodate the child and that the child meets any pre-existing entrance requirements such as religious affiliation or ability. This freedom of choice depends on two crucial factors: first, there must be enough schools locally for the choice to be exercised; and, second, the parents must have the resources (such as time and finance) to transport the child to the chosen school. Certain schools will still retain a near monopoly position because if there are no other local schools conveniently available, then parents have no effective choice. The nature of the catchment area may also mean that, even where choice exists, the convenience of a local school overcomes broader educational factors. What impact does open enrolment have on marketing a school? In this new environment, marketing to attract and retain pupils gains a much higher profile, whether schools have a near monopoly position and are only affected at the margin or whether they are in a much more competitive position.

The significance of open enrolment can be seen in Fig 1.1 which shows that an increase or decrease in pupil numbers as a result of parents operating their power of choice has, through the formula-funding mechanism, a direct effect on the financial viability of schools. A school at point A will be spending 70 per cent of its budget on variable costs (such as teachers, books and equipment) and 30 per cent of its budget on fixed costs (which are mainly premises-related). If the school gains pupils, the money which the pupils bring in will not have to be spent on fixed costs (as the buildings are already maintained) and most of it can be spent on teachers, books and equipment. Thus, at point B, although the school spends the same amount on its fixed costs, these costs are now a smaller proportion of total costs. The reverse is true when a school loses pupils. Although it receives less money it still has to meet its fixed costs. As a result, these fixed costs take up a bigger share of the budget, leaving less to be spent on the variable costs of teachers and materials. This can be seen at point C which reflects the fall in income due to a decline in pupil numbers.

While this is a simplified version of the complex nature of school costs it does demonstrate the impact of open enrolment and market forces on those costs. The market mechanism was introduced at a time when rolls, in secondary schools at least, were so low that many schools had spare capacity and were

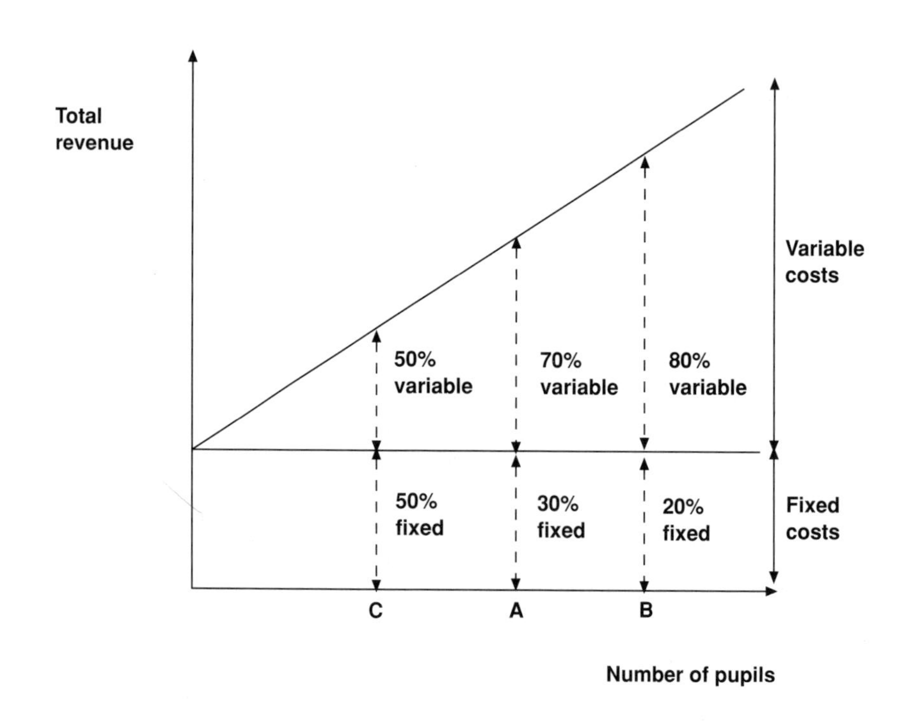

Figure 1.1 Cost relationships with formula-based funding

able to accommodate pupils from other areas. This type of situation reinforces the need for effective marketing.

With formula funding and open enrolments, therefore, the movement of pupils between schools can have a very significant effect on budgets. Expanding schools are able to spend much of their income on teachers and materials and so attract more pupils. The reverse is true of declining schools which have less money but which must spend proportionately more on fixed costs. This emphasises the point that Local Management of Schools (LMS) and Grant-maintained Status (GMS) are not just financial changes but that they radically alter the nature of the education system and the educational market. While the main reason that a school *should* be marketing is a desire to improve its service and relationship with its clients, the main reason why it *has* to market itself is that, in the late 1990s and the new millennium, economic realities make this a precondition of its future survival. There is no point in having a quality product and having a belief that it is desirable if the message is not communicated and the school does not continue to exist.

To whom are schools marketing?

If marketing a school centres on the concept of effective communication, then it is vital to have a clear view of the target audience. A simplistic view would be to look only at the immediate recipients of the school's work – the parent and child – especially when one considers the implications of formula funding and open enrolment. However, this approach ignores the broader set of stakeholders (both internal and external) who are, for a variety of reasons, also significant in marketing terms. It may be helpful at this point to clarify some of the terminology which abounds in the field of marketing when referring to the stakeholders. The terms 'consumer', 'customer' and 'client' are used in different ways by different people. While we do not believe that there is a need to be pedantic about the differences, we will use the following definitions.

- *The consumer*. This is the direct recipient of the products and services of the school. This is usually the pupil, but for the wider functions of the school such as a curriculum information session or a staff development activity, the focus shifts to the parent or member of staff as the consumer.
- *The customer*. This is the person who makes the decision to buy. This would normally be the parents and child as they choose a school or a particular set of options within it. In the case of private or charity-run special schools, for example, it could be an LEA which is deciding whether or not to buy places for the pupils who have a particular special need. Again there are some broader interpretations of the term 'customer' – for example, when a candidate for a post decides whether or not to proceed with an application or to accept the post.

- *The client.* This all-embracing term can be used to include those falling into the consumer or customer categories and all those who are beneficiaries or potential beneficiaries, either directly or indirectly, of the work of the school.

Schools do not exist to provide teachers with jobs; they exist to provide effective education. It is, therefore, an essential prerequisite for the effective marketing of schools that staff should reflect on the nature of the various client groups. The very broad range of these groups, from industry and commerce to local charities, needs to be broken down by the process of market segmentation so that a school can relate effectively to each group. Traditionally, market segmentation is a way of dividing clients and potential clients into groups within which there are identical needs. However, because of the diversity of expectations from the education service, it is more realistic to consider that the clients in a segment would have broadly similar, rather than identical, needs. If this concept of market segmentation is applied to schools, the grouping shown in Table 1.1 could result.

Table 1.1 Market segmentation in the education sector

Internal markets	*External markets*
• Governors	• Prospective pupils
• Staff (teaching and support)	• Prospective parents
• Regular visitors and helpers	• Former pupils
• Current pupils	• Prospective staff
• Current parents	• Other educational institutions
	• The local community
	• Commerce and industry
	• The Local Education Authority/Funding Agency
	• The Office for Standards in Education
	• The Teacher Training Agency/General Teaching Council
	• National groups and organisations

The clear identification of these market segments and the importance of effective communication with them will be discussed in Chapter Seven.

What are schools marketing?

The discussion which follows is not just about the various values and attainments which a school puts across; it takes a different view, examining the significance of both overt and covert performance indicators. Many schools fail to recognise the distinction between these. Do people choose a school because of its test/examination results and other similar quantifiable factors? Certainly these are significant factors, especially at secondary level, but the reputation of a school is made up of a series of complex and inter-related factors. Wearing school uniform, which parents associate with good discipline, and the amount of homework, which they associate with academic standards, can be very significant. The reputation of many schools may be enhanced by the overt reality of good staff/pupil relationships and high academic standards. However, this reputation can be undone by the behaviour of pupils in the local town at lunchtime or when travelling on school buses and by pupils smoking outside the school gates. These determinants of the perceptions which parents have of the school are often more important than the reality of what is actually going on in the delivery of effective education.

A useful management exercise for school staff to undertake is to list four strengths and weaknesses of the school as they perceive them (an exercise described in Chapter Eight). Then they should draw on the knowledge gained from the interaction which they have, for example, with parents at parents' meetings, in order to list the strengths and weaknesses as perceived by parents. The key management task involves comparing the two lists. It is not only the teachers in the school who set the criteria; there may be significant factors in the perceptions of parents which determine the reputation of a school but which have little to do with its core educational activities.

Schools, therefore, have to consider whether they might be concentrating on marketing a set of values which parents take for granted, while ignoring a number of factors which parents perceive as being key indicators of a 'good' school. While we would not suggest that fundamental educational values are ignored at the expense of marketing pragmatism, it is vital that staff do not assume that they know what parents regard as significant indicators of a school's success. If they are to fulfil their educational mission, schools must address the concerns of their clients and respond to them. The only way to do this is to sample parental opinion to find out what is considered to be significant rather than to rely on the existing teacher perceptions based within the internal culture of the school. This process is explored in Chapter Eight.

Any response to client wants must be a genuine one. The image projected must reflect the product and service which a school actually delivers. If a false view is conveyed, it will not be long before the various client groups will realise that they have been misled.

Myths and misconceptions about marketing

There are various myths and misconceptions about marketing in the educational world, one of which has already been highlighted – namely, the idea that it is a rather disreputable activity. Some others are discussed in the sections which follow.

Misconception 1 Marketing is merely about promoting the school

Very often schools see marketing as designing a new school prospectus or a new school sign. These promotional activities are, in fact, only part of the process of marketing. What is more important is that schools realise that the staff, and all those involved with the school, should understand the nature and scope of marketing as a concept. One of the central concerns of marketing is quality. The marketing of schools involves finding out what the clients want and need (now and in the foreseeable future) and then designing a product and service which provides a quality education to meet those wants and needs. The concept of marketing is rooted in an organisational orientation which focuses on client wants and needs and on their satisfaction. It is concerned with the benefits derived by the client rather than the features provided by the supplier. In essence, marketing can be seen as the key element in the accountability and responsibility relationship which the school has with its clients. The school should, therefore, communicate effectively the fact that it is providing the product/service which meets the wants and needs of its clients.

Schools should see marketing as being the way that they think about and respond to their clients and not as being a single event such as producing a prospectus. The distinction has to be drawn between these single events and the overall marketing process. Marketing is thus best thought of as a *process* and not an *event*.

Misconception 2 Marketing is only to people outside the school

Another misconception about marketing is that it is concerned solely with external relationships, especially the promotion of an image of the school to the outside world. It is important to realise that there are both internal and external markets (*see* Table 1.1) and it is the internal one which needs to be given attention initially. If those inside the school do not have a clear sense of its purpose, identity and values then it will be difficult to convince the external world of these characteristics. If individuals from the external community meet teachers, pupils and governors and perceive that they have no clear idea of what the school stands for or of its successes and achievements, then it will cast doubt on the reliability of any promotional or publicity information which they have received.

In order to communicate an effective message, the pupils, staff (teaching and support) and governors must have a corporate perspective. For this reason, the initial marketing activity must concentrate on those working inside the school. They need to develop a coherent view of the school, agreeing and supporting the aims and values, before any external marketing is undertaken. It is the quality of the 'internal product' that will effectively enhance the reputation of the school in the long run. There is little point in looking at external marketing and promotion strategies unless a coherent internal educational structure and commitment exists. In our experience many schools do exactly the opposite by concentrating on the external market first.

Misconception 3 Marketing is 'not our job'

One of the most difficult things to change in an organisation is individuals' attitudes. It is especially difficult to change the way in which people think about marketing because of its historical development in the industrial/ commercial world. Everyone inside the school, such as teachers, caretakers and secretaries, should act as ambassadors for the school and should fulfil this role when they respond to individuals or to organisations. The problem is that, too often, marketing is seen to be the sole responsibility of senior management. Traditionally, teachers have seen their job as getting on with teaching and, similarly, office staff and other support staff focus on the task in hand. However, the clients, when they assess a school, often make judgements based on the representatives whom they meet when contacting the school for the first time. This may be the school secretary who answers the telephone or the teacher whom they meet after school. It is important for all staff to see that they have a role in presenting a positive view of the school and that they should seek opportunities to do so.

The traditional view of schools as being ivory towers where parents and community are kept at 'arm's length' by the professionals who guard 'knowledge and culture' does not always project a welcoming image to current or prospective clients. School signs which display 'parents are not allowed beyond this point' are not totally unknown! They say more about the organisation's view of its relationship with the outside community than any rhetoric in the school prospectus. This traditional attitude has to be replaced by one where everyone accepts that it is their task to represent and market the school.

Misconception 4 The wants and needs of the clients are the same

We have already identified the various client groups that make up the 'market' of the school but in this section we use parents and children as an example to demonstrate the difference between wants and needs. There is a problem to be faced concerning the balance between the educational needs of children and the wants articulated by them or their parents. If schools are to relate their services to the wants and needs of the clients, then a dilemma may present itself because the wants as perceived by the clients may not match the pupils' needs as perceived by the professional educators.

The definition used in this book is that *wants* are things which parents and children desire or demand in terms of educational services, whereas *needs* are those educational experiences and values which professional educators and society in general determine that children require at different stages of their development. Obviously, these wants and needs may not coincide at any particular moment.

If schools were to take the view that 'the customer is always right' and to try to meet the very diverse wants of individuals, then the result would probably be a chaotic and unsatisfactory educational experience for the pupils. There are, for example, very differing views of the school's role in sex education. An alternative approach to reconciling wants and needs is required. The real art in effective management is to lead clients towards a situation where their expectations coincide with those of the school. On this basis, therefore, a school must provide an education in which content and quality both meet the needs of pupils as identified by professional educators and society and, as far as possible, satisfy the wants as identified by the pupils and their parents.

This can only happen when the clients are sure that the professionals understand their preferences and perceptions about the nature of the educational product or service. However, it should be realised that perceptions are not fixed. They can be changed by the actions of professionals. Teachers should, therefore, be striving to assist their clients to a more sophisticated interpretation of the product or service and of the school's success criteria in line with those that they would use as professionals.

It is this view of meeting needs and wants in an accountability relationship and the effective communication of the school's values, activities and achievements which are central to the concept of marketing. Such organisational understanding needs to precede the detailed management of the process of marketing.

Misconception 5 Either the pupil or the parent is the immediate client

Having established the difference between wants and needs it is important to examine whose wants and needs are being considered. Is it the pupil or the parent who is the immediate client? The pupil/parent dimension of client identification is one which gives rise to a number of misconceptions and is a key issue for schools to explore. The 1988 Education Reform Act sees the parent as the 'customer' exercising rights through a policy of increased choice. However, in practice, it is not as simple as this.

In the primary school most staff would see the pupils as the clients and, therefore, the first priority of the teacher. On the other hand, secondary school teachers often consider that the parents are the clients and that they are accountable to them. This view can be considered further by assessing decisions about the choice of school. Using this as a criterion, the conclusion could be that the parent is the client when the child is younger and that the pupil becomes the client as he/she grows up. It is true that the younger the child, the more dominant is the parent in making the choice of school. As children grow older and attend secondary school and, more significantly, when they move into post-16 education, they play a more dominant role in the choice process. It would be wrong, however, to take the simplistic view that the parent is the client with an increasing role being undertaken by the child as he/she grows older. At different stages and to differing degrees the child and parent influence each other as to the value and esteem in which the school is held. When the child goes home and relates good or bad experiences about the school, this influences parental opinion and, in turn, the parental response influences the child's perception of the school.

While it is important to maintain an awareness of both pupil and parent wants, attention should also be focused on the deliberate transmission of positive images to the clients – a significant aspect of managing a school's reputation and one which involves all the staff every day. Pupils should go home with a clear view of the purpose of the school and of the activities which take place so that parents feel confident about the quality of education provided. Parents should also be made aware, by more direct contact, of the school's aims and of the approaches which are being used to achieve these. If pupils and parents are committed to the school then they will reinforce each other's positive views and will act as ambassadors for the school in the wider community.

It is, therefore, necessary to reconsider the question 'Who is the immediate client?' Perhaps it is preferable to see this not as an 'either/or' situation but as an integration of pupil and parental wants where a balance of interests should be met. As outlined in the previous section, those wants then have to be reconciled with the educational needs. Viewing both the parent and the pupil as the immediate client is not fudging the issue but is maintaining the fine balance which schools must achieve in building effective relationships with their clients.

Education markets as allocation systems

Marketing should not be confused with markets as distribution systems. Having looked at marketing as an activity, it is now appropriate briefly to consider markets as a means of allocating resources. Markets in the business and industrial world are based on the premise that individuals or organisations determine what is produced and sold by the seemingly unco-ordinated actions of buyers and sellers. If buyers demand a particular 'good' then suppliers will, in turn, buy raw materials and labour and borrow capital in the expectation that they can make that good and sell it at a profit. Thus the distribution of goods and services is dependent on the relative prices that buyers are prepared to pay and suppliers are prepared to accept. Simple supply and demand analysis would suggest that suppliers want as high a price as possible and that buyers will purchase more at lower prices. The balance between the two is the market price which determines the amount bought and sold.

In the wider international economy, market systems have replaced central planning systems, as has been seen with the collapse of the Soviet empire and the adoption of market reforms in such countries as China. In the UK context, market forces – often referred to as 'the discipline of the market' – have been applied to the public sector and, in particular, to education. However, by definition, public goods which are paid for by one group of people (taxpayers), often consumed by a different group of people (service consumers) and allocated by criteria other than price, cannot easily be considered to be fully market-orientated. Let us take the case of education over the last ten years.

The education reforms in the UK and overseas have had a number of common themes.

- A centralised curriculum can be considered as a means of informing 'customers' about the nature of the product that they are buying.
- The associated standardised tests provide 'benchmarks' of performance so that the publication of examination and standardised test results and other information are means of informing the 'customers' about the quality of what they are buying.
- Parental choice of schools, when combined with the linking of school funding to the number of pupils on the roll, is the means of allocating resources to schools by choice mechanisms.

In practice what has happened is that there are only a limited number of school places which are allocated by factors such as price. Local capacity, in terms of places at individual schools, is not very flexible and is allocated on administrative criteria. Furthermore, information is still limited, thus constraining parental choice. These limitations are summed up by Levačić:

> *Given that state school places are rationed by administrative criteria and not by price, schools with desirable characteristics as perceived by parents and with insufficient places to meet demand are over-subscribed, since excess demand is not rationed by price as in a normal market.* (Levačić, 1995, p25)

However, she concludes:

> *For all its deficiencies of structure and information, the school quasi-market has become more competitive through more open enrolment in the context of surplus places in many areas, and parents now have more information, particularly if they choose to seek it out.* (Levačić, 1995, p26)

We can conclude that markets are about allocative systems through which resources are distributed to organisations and goods to individuals. In the education sector we can say that market reforms have introduced several elements of market forces so we have 'part-markets', or what the economists often call 'quasi-markets'. This provides the contextual setting in which schools operate. Within this context, individual schools may or may not choose to engage in marketing themselves. However, as we have shown in the earlier part of this chapter, choosing the *right* marketing strategy rather than choosing whether to market or not is the more appropriate decision for most schools.

Conclusion

This chapter has sought to describe the nature of marketing within an educational context. Chapter Two looks at the strategic stages that we use in this book – creating strategic intent, undertaking a strategic analysis and marketing implementation. It will then consider some key points to aid the successful 'process management' of marketing the school.

References

Davies, B. and Ellison, L. (1997) *School Leadership for the 21st Century*, London, Routledge.

DES (1988) *The Education Reform Act*, London, HMSO.

Levačić, R. (1995) *Local Management of Schools*, Buckingham, Open University Press.

2

The Process of Marketing

How you manage is as important as what you manage

Introduction

Marketing is too often thought of as a single event or as a series of techniques and approaches. This causes those responsible for marketing to engage (mistakenly) in reactive responses without a clear framework for action. To avoid this we think it important to take a wider perspective on marketing within the context of a strategic view of the school's development. We have been very impressed by an excellent book edited by Bob Garratt *Developing Strategic Thought* (1995) and in particular a chapter written by Max Boisot called 'Preparing for turbulence: the changing relationship between strategy and management development in the learning organisation'. We have used one of Boisot's models to develop the fundamental framework in this book.

We have adapted Boisot's model and focused on two of the four domains that he outlines – those of *strategic intent* and *strategic planning* (*see* Fig 2.1). In the figure, one axis relates to the degree of turbulence and hence change in the environment and the second to the level of understanding that an organisation has of the turbulence and change in which it exists. Once the two dimensions have been considered, appropriate management responses can then be activated.

1 *Strategic intent* is described by Boisot as 'a process of coping with turbulence through a direct, intuitive understanding, emanating from the top of the firm and guiding its efforts' (1995, p36). He goes on to suggest that an organisation 'operating in a regime of strategic intent can use a common vision to keep the behaviour of its employees aligned with a common purpose …' (1995, p37). Translating this into an educational context we would suggest that a school which is dealing with either a longer-term timeframe or a less predictable marketing environment needs to build in all of its staff a common strategic intent based on the values, aims and

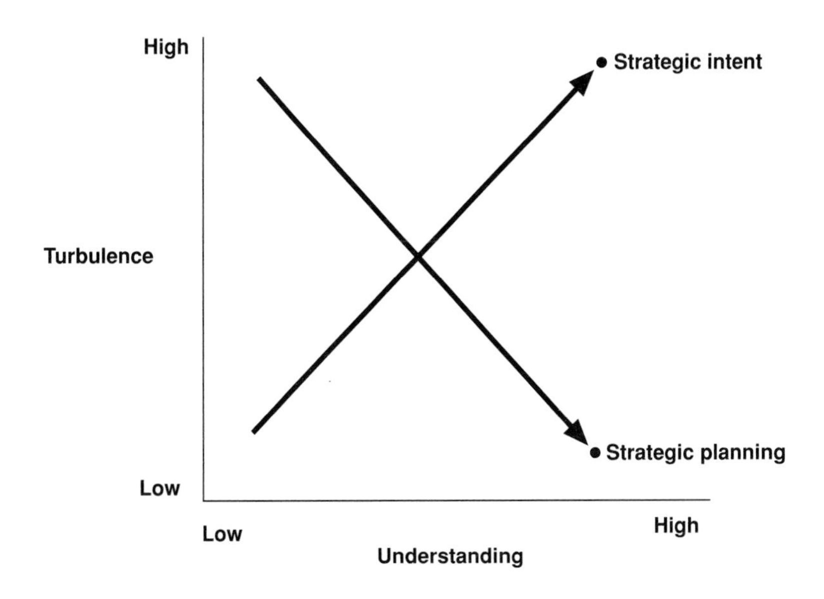

Figure 2.1 Typology of strategies
Source: After Boisot, 1995, p40; reproduced by permission of the publisher, McGraw Hill Books UK Ltd, McGraw Hill House, Shoppenhangers Road, Maidenhead SL6 2QL

ambitions of the school which all staff can articulate and to which they can align themselves. Thus, faced with new and untried situations they can draw on that common understanding as a frame of reference.

2 *Strategic planning* is effective in an environment in which the rate of change is slower than the rate at which the organisation can understand and adapt to it. In such a case, the fact that marketing processes can be planned and put into action and the results evaluated in a reasonably consistent and planned manner is due to one of two factors:

   - the environment is one which is related to the shorter-term, more predictable environment; or,
   - the nature of the activity being marketed is traditional or incremental and not subject to significant turbulence or change.

   A school in such a situation can have a clear strategic plan for the definable part of its activities and for its marketing.

The environment in which schools must operate in the late 1990s and early in the next millennium is more like that described as requiring strategic intent, and so it is this environment which we address first in this book. However, once the strategic intent has been established, some of the tools from strategic planning can be usefully adapted to take the marketing process forward in the short to medium term. The components of the marketing process will now be outlined so that they can be developed in the rest of the book. This chapter goes on to explain that the marketing process is set within the context of a range of key elements which constitute the marketing mix. It concludes by summarising some of the key factors which we have found to contribute to the effective marketing of schools.

The components of the marketing process

Marketing should not be considered as an individual event but as a process that is part of an overall management strategy. In this book we consider that there are three main phases to this marketing process, each with its own sub-sections. These are shown in Fig 2.2.

One of the potential failures of marketing in schools is to start at implementation rather than to follow the cyclical process as outlined above and another is to fail to realise the significance of the inter-relationships between each of the phases.

1 *Strategic intent* is the process of binding all those engaged in the school to a focused and directed purpose (*see* Fig 2.3). It is the bedrock on which a marketing strategy is built. If those working in the school cannot articulate its purpose and aims, its core values and its achievements and demonstrate their belief in them, then many of the marketing techniques and approaches will be seen as superficial and may be ineffective as the clients could be

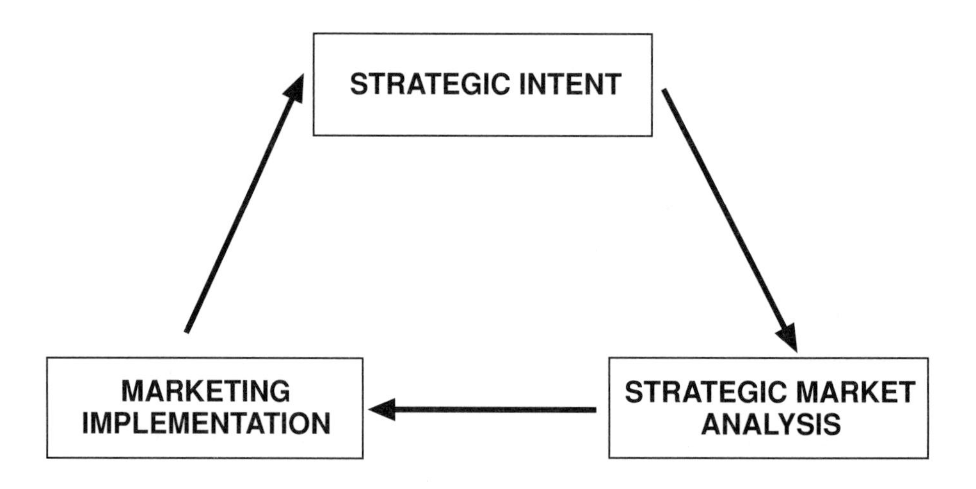

Figure 2.2 The phases of the marketing process

Figure 2.3 The concepts within strategic intent

faced with a discrepancy between the image of the school and the reality of their experience when coming into contact with the school community. In Part Two we build on the ideas of Kawasaki (1995) and suggest that creating a strategic intent involves the three linked concepts of a strategic cause, a client-focused culture and a pro-active staff.

2 *Strategic market analysis* is mainly concerned with market research into a number of key areas: the school's environment, its competitors, its clients, its product and service (*see* Fig 2.4 overleaf). When this analysis has been carried out, the school's senior managers need to integrate and interpret the evidence obtained before they can make decisions about implementing a marketing strategy. This is described in Part Three of the book.

3 *Marketing implementation* (*see* Fig 2.5 on page 21) comprises three major parts: assessing the techniques and approaches available for marketing; implementing a marketing plan to promote the school; and, finally, evaluating the effectiveness of the overall marketing process. These are explained in Part Four.

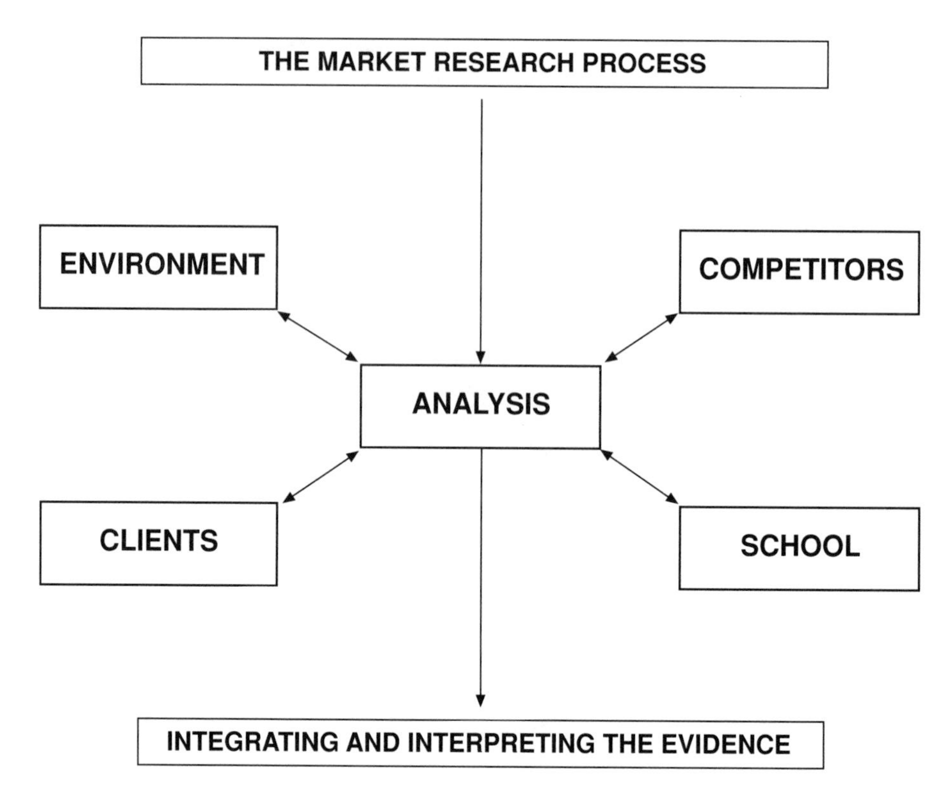

Figure 2.4 The processes within strategic market analysis

The context of the marketing process: the marketing mix

The process of marketing is based around a number of key elements that will be developed throughout the book. Often referred to as the marketing mix, we can list these as *product, price, place, people, promotion* and *positioning*. These elements form the link between the organisation and the clients.

Product

Product is obviously the education service provided to the pupils and is the most significant aspect of the marketing mix. Using business terms such as 'product' for education does seem rather harsh on the one hand, but on the other hand it provides a distinctive framework within which to analyse our activities. It can usefully be broken down into four components: *product range, product benefits, product life* and *product quality*.

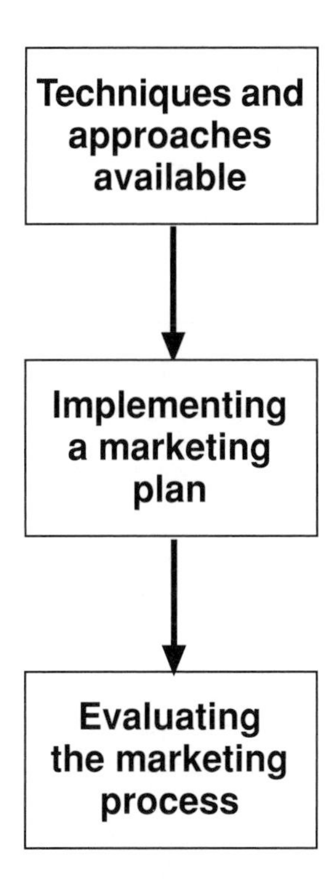

Figure 2.5 The stages within marketing implementation

1 *Product range.* In the business world, product range would be the range of goods and services offered to the customer. In education it refers mainly to the nature and extent of the curriculum supported by a wide range of extra-curricular activities and other services. While it is true that the national curriculum is making the product range similar across schools, there is also considerable scope for differentiation. Some primary schools offer nursery provision or after-school care while others offer specialist computer or music provision. In the secondary phase the range of subjects taught at GCSE and at 'A' level can be critical in forming the decision about choice of school, as can GNVQ provision or links with further and higher education. In all sectors, the nature of the provision for those with special educational needs can be a significant factor in clients' decision-making. Similarly, the school's particular ethos or the nature of the education provided, whether based on a religious denomination or other cultural factors, can be a key factor in defining the product for the clients.

2 *Product benefits.* This is a more nebulous concept and focuses on the benefits obtained from the education process rather than the process itself. For example, if a pupil obtains good examination results but is unable to gain a job then the benefits derived from the school may be viewed as being

limited. This may be considered the end-use benefit rather than the intrinsic value of the education. Although we are used to describing the process rather than the benefits, in recent years there has been a switch in mentality to a wider range of performance indicators and to output-based budgets rather than just considering inputs. In marketing terms, it is important for the school to convey the benefits of the outcomes as well as the educational processes involved.

3 *Product life.* It is easy to understand the concept of product life in a commercial or retail setting where new goods come onto the shelf and then are later replaced by more advanced models. In the same way elements of the curriculum are revised, adapted or radically changed. This is also true of the learning process, especially when considering information technology and its use in schools. In marketing terms, having a vision of the future needs of the pupils and the appropriate curricular and learning strategies enables the school to be at the forefront of educational and market development.

4 *Product quality.* It is of paramount importance to know how pupils and parents, as well as the wider client community, determine or define quality. Chapter Eight pays particular attention to analysing clients' opinions and to obtaining their view of quality instead of those determined solely by the supplier (the school). This quality may be perceived in overt ways such as through published test/examination results but can also, most importantly, be seen through covert factors such as school-gate 'gossip' or pupils' behaviour outside school.

Price

It is simplistic to consider that price is only applicable to the physical goods market. Price is obviously a key factor in the private sector of education where parents are paying different fee levels at different schools. Some parents will make choices between private fee-paying schools and what they consider 'good' state schools. It is also noticeable that some parents 'mix and match' private and state schools at different stages of their child's education or 'top-up' state provision, for example through individual music tuition or examination coaching. The concept of 'price' can also be seen from the school's perspective because the introduction of formula-led funding linked directly to pupil numbers has meant that each pupil has a price. Schools, while not in a free market, are in a quasi-market and can expand various parts of their activity after considering the cost and revenue implications. Certainly the introduction in 1996 of vouchers for nursery education has expanded provision and has brought cost/price considerations overtly into this sector of the market.

Place

This is the geographical and physical location of the school in terms of its convenience or accessibility to clients and also internal factors such as its appearance and condition as well as the 'feel'. These latter aspects are very significant. While parents and pupils do not make decisions solely on one factor, getting them 'through the door' to see the quality of what is going on inside the school is the first hurdle. Thus, attractive buildings with welcoming facilities in a convenient location certainly help! A very valuable exercise is to use governors or parents who are new to the school to give an outsider's or newcomer's view of initial impressions.

People

A significant factor in education is that a large proportion of the educational product is delivered through the people in the school. Thus, a key determinant of the success of the educational marketing effort is the people in terms of their motivation and quality. This is discussed in Chapter Three where we consider the importance of creating a strategic intent within the people in the school, focusing on the need to draw up, sustain and communicate the vision and the purpose of the school.

Promotion

There are a number of techniques and approaches that can be employed to convey the intent of the school, the educational activities and the benefits of the product. These techniques and approaches include such things as communication via publications, the media and the people associated with the school. These are described in more detail in Chapter Ten.

Positioning

In industry and commerce a great deal of attention is given to market positioning. It can best be considered as the way that your clients perceive your organisation in the marketplace. 'Traditional', 'responsive', 'academic', 'caring', 'good extra-curricular provision', 'high quality special needs provision', 'good discipline', 'strong moral values', 'a religious ethos' are all descriptions which clients use when talking about schools. In a sense they are identifying a school as having a clear reputation for a specific group of attributes which define its position in the educational market.

Key factors in the success of the marketing process

There are a number of key factors in the marketing process that increase the chances of a successful outcome. We summarise some that we have come across in our work with schools and which we have found useful in developing an effective and appropriate marketing strategy for a school.

1 *Avoid confusing strategy with tactics.* As we have mentioned earlier, rushing into a marketing effort without a clear set of objectives or a well thought-out approach can lead to ineffective marketing and a significant waste of resources. There is a considerable difference between reacting to other schools' marketing efforts or other people's agendas and developing your own strategy and setting your own agenda. The latter focuses on the school being a strategically pro-active organisation rather than a reactive organisation.

2 *Avoid lack of planning.* Plan the planning time! Time for reflection and discussion should be built into the planning process so that simplistic solutions are avoided. The key elements in effective communication with the clients must be considered, tested and adjusted before the final strategy is adopted. The time pressures in schools and the frequent desire to make decisions or achieve solutions quickly mean that there is the danger that they will be the wrong decisions or the wrong solutions if insufficient attention is given to discussing the full implications or the alternative solutions. Our approach to planning the sequence of marketing activities is described in Chapter Eleven.

3 *Avoid lack of focus.* The problem is usually 'too much and too much detail'! There are three things that a good marketing strategy needs and these are focus, focus and focus! The more objectives or activities that are undertaken, the more likely it is that the marketing effort will become diluted. Focusing on a limited number of issues and employing focused strategies is likely to lead to greater success. Marketing should not be seen as a one-off event but a series of activities over time. As such these should be sequenced and paced and not undertaken all at once. Too much information can be confusing whereas a clear and simple message that is reinforced by a wide range of people and sources is likely to be very effective.

4 *Manage the marketing culture as well as the marketing activities in the school.* The central mission for schools is that they should provide the highest quality education possible. Nothing in this book suggests that this mission does not or should not remain as a central focus. If the school provides high quality education, then marketing is the proud display of that quality. Marketing therefore should not be considered as one of those management functions that only concern a few people and has little to do with the work of the school. It sits side by side with the educational process and must be integrated into the school's work and culture. We need to promote

positively the concept of marketing so that the staff of the school and the parents and pupils recognise, accept and believe in its significance. All staff need to be convinced that this is something in which they need to be actively involved; they need to become 'ambassadors' of the school. As with a number of innovations and changes in a school, the chance of success may depend not necessarily on the context or the nature of the change but on how it is managed. This illustrates the well-known management maxim that 'the way that you manage the change is as important as the change itself'.

5 *Incorporate marketing into the school development planning process.* Short-, medium- and long-term plans should involve a marketing strategy for managing the school's reputation and promoting its aims, goals and activities. Marketing should not be 'bolted-on' to other management activities. It should not be considered as an afterthought but as an integral part of an activity. The way that we communicate and promote the activities which the school undertakes should be a consideration at the design stage and not the implementation stage. (This subject is covered in greater depth in another title in this series, *Strategic Development Planning for Schools* (Davies and Ellison, 1997).)

6 *Develop an outward-facing and not an inward-looking school.* Schools need to relate to the communities which they serve and staff should look to taking the quality of what they do out to the market and promoting it. They must realise that it is their responsibility to change perceptions of the school in the wider world. All too often professional educators have not communicated effectively what they are doing or seen the necessity to do so. As a result politicians and other parties have filled the vacuum and dictated the educational agenda. To reverse this trend we need to lose some of the traditional reserve associated with the public sector and be far more pro-active in communicating and linking with the wider community. We should not be apologetic about marketing. We should take the initiative and put across positive images of the school. This can be done in an ethical as well as an effective way. Communicating and promoting the school's aims and achievements also reinforces a positive image for those working inside the school.

7 *Promote the concept and practice of the responsive school.* Schools should be market-orientated and not product-orientated, user-orientated and not provider-orientated, client-driven and not organisation-driven. This means that those involved in the development and operation of the school should take a strategic view of client wants and needs and should also be responsive to the needs and opinions of clients as expressed on a day-to-day basis (a theme which is followed up in Chapter Three).

PART TWO

■ ■ ■

Strategic Intent

3 **Creating Strategic Intent** *29*

3

Creating Strategic Intent

One person with a belief is equal to a force of ninety-nine who only have an interest (John Stuart Mill)

Introduction

In this chapter we will deal with creating the strategic intent which was suggested in Chapter 2 to be the most appropriate starting point in the marketing of schools. This strategic intent might be considered as establishing both vision and culture. We move on in future chapters to see how the common understandings thus formed can be used in planning the school's future and in its marketing process.

The building of a strategic intent, with a common sense of vision and an appropriate culture, is a precondition of other phases of the marketing process. We consider that the building of strategic intent involves three stages.

1. Creating a strategic cause.
2. Creating a client-focused culture.
3. Creating a pro-active staff.

Creating a strategic cause

Kawasaki (1995, p89), in his excellent ideas book on marketing, uses a quote from John Stuart Mill 'One person with a belief is equal to a force of ninety-nine who only have an interest'. We find this very profound and it underpins a perspective which we articulate several times in this book – that is, that no matter what positive communication is directed out from the school, if the clients or prospective clients obtain a different reaction when they come into contact with the teachers and pupils, not only will the original efforts be nullified but, worse, they will feel that they have been 'conned'.

One of the most powerful examples in a business context came from Jan Carlzon of Scandinavian Air Services (SAS) who used the term 'moment of truth'. He saw that each brief encounter between an employee and a customer defined the reality of the customer's perception of the company. If the customer saw someone who believed in the company and extolled its virtues then that belief could be transferred to the customer. Conversely, if in that 'moment of truth' a negative image was conveyed, then there would be a significant adverse effect on the organisation and its image.

Although the examples used by Kawasaki (1995) about creating a 'cause' are from business they have qualities that are transferable to education. He defines a cause as 'something you believe in and want others to believe in as much as you do' (1995, p90). He then sets out four characteristics for creating a successful cause – that a cause: embodies a vision; seizes the high ground; redefines experiences; and catalyses strong feelings. We will now apply these to an educational setting.

1 *A cause embodies a vision.* Vision and mission statements have been much over-used in management courses for schools but the concept of a future-orientated focus is vital for success. The alternative to having a vision is a reactive organisation that is either cruising or strolling along with no long-term picture to guide it. A vision articulates a clear sense of purpose and is by definition future-oriented. It sets out the hopes and aspirations of the school for children, community and staff. The writings of Jenkins (1991) and Fullan (1993) are very useful here. Jenkins (1991, p38) defines vision as:

   > *... an interpretation of the direction in which the organisation is going – an interpretation which inspires and illuminates and permeates the organisation.*

2 *A cause seizes the high ground.* It embodies and articulates a clear set of shared values that are aimed at significantly improving the pupils' experiences and achievements.

3 *A cause redefines experiences.* It seeks new interpretations and new ways of doing things. It is about not being satisfied with the current state of affairs and searching out better solutions. This reflects Bennis and Nanus' view of a vision as something which:

   > *... articulates a view of a realistic, credible, attractive future for the organisation, a condition that is better in some important ways than what now exists* (1985, p89)

4 *A cause catalyses strong feelings.* It makes people want to belong and 'buy into the vision'. For example, pupils enjoy being at the school and are proud of its achievements. Parents and other client groups 'buy into the vision', enthusiastically supporting both the school's core provision and its wider activities.

When creating a strategic cause, one of the key questions to address which may at first seem rather banal is 'What business are you in?' This should then be followed by the question 'What business do you want to be in?' Answering the question as 'schooling' or 'education' is superficial. Making more sophisticated analyses like transmitting basic skills, love of learning, cultural understanding and the ability to work with others may start to define current experiences.

Creating a client-focused culture

The most difficult part of marketing a school is not necessarily just adapting or operationalising the key stages in the school marketing plan but it is the establishment of a marketing culture within the school. It is important to examine some of the critical concepts in moving the attitude of school leaders and staff from being product-orientated to being more client-orientated. In order to be more effective, this organisational understanding must precede the detailed management of the marketing process. This section is organised into seven parts which focus on the issues in the development of this client-focused culture:

- The importance of the client
- Responding to clients
- Never letting the client down
- One impression of the school or many?
- Ensuring that the school provides a service as well as a product
- The management of a high quality service approach
- Developing a client-based philosophy.

The importance of the client

Chapter One discussed client identification in education, examining the pupil/parent relationship and the concept of the wider community as a client of the school. The way that clients have been perceived by schools to date may be considerably different from the way that a commercial or industrial company would regard a client. While in the business world the idea of being client-orientated or of 'putting the customer first' is commonplace, such an attitude can seem somewhat out of place in education. The culture of schools has traditionally centred on their being the source of knowledge and their transmitting this knowledge to a captive audience. The result has been a product-orientation where knowledge and skills have predominated. However, much can be learned from commerce and industry. Raising these issues and applying some of the business concepts can provide a useful stimulus to the educational debate concerning the ways in which we think about clients.

The following statements should provide a discussion framework:

- The client is the most important person in the school and the quality of the contact, in person, in writing or by telephone is the key to a successful relationship.
- A client comes to us for education; we should provide this (the service) in a way that delivers a professional product which satisfies both the wants and needs of the client.
- The client is not something that is additional to the school; without the client there is no school.
- Clients do not interrupt our work; they are our work.
- Whereas the client may be dependent on us for providing an education, we are dependent on the client for our jobs.

If used with staff groups, this sort of thinking is quite powerful in that it enables them to address the way in which they perceive clients and the importance of client relationships to the school. Such challenges to existing patterns of thinking are necessary in order to move schools into becoming market-orientated. This book does not argue that we should forget the traditional values of schools in favour of just considering clients' wants, but it argues very strongly that the knowledge and skills in the schools should be orientated both to meet those wants, and to meet the identified needs of the clients. This means that we must rethink our view of the client and adopt a client-orientation. The school and the client are not separate; the clients are part of the school, if not *the* school itself.

Responding to clients

Clients expect to be treated seriously, courteously, with concern and with problem-solving, rather than blame-attaching, attitudes. In industry, staff at all levels undertake training on how to deal with clients on a face-to-face basis and on the telephone, but in education we are usually left to learn by 'trial and error'. Developing experience this way has, on the majority of occasions, worked quite well but there are exceptions. When it does not work well there are problems with the trial-and-error approach – it can be a *trial* for the client because we make *errors*!

A good example of how we treat clients is provided by examining what happens when the telephone is answered. Is the response, 'Good morning, Brentwich School. Can I help you?' or is it just a curt 'Yes!'? Do we respond 'The headteacher is working with children and we always give that priority in this school, but she will telephone you later' or 'The headteacher's not around. Can you try later?'

Another example is found in the management of parents' meetings. How do we train teachers to communicate with parents so that the teachers' expectations and parents' expectations meet and both go away satisfied with the encounter? The truth is that we spend little or, more often, no time in training staff in meeting the clients' expectations and handling the communication exchange with them. Yet in business 'customer care' courses are commonplace.

Clients expect their problems to be solved and do not expect to be told that there are so many internal procedures which prevent a solution. While, in the real world, it is not possible to meet the often contradictory wants of different groups of parents, the *attitude* with which staff tackle the problems and look for positive solutions is often the factor which parents remember. This is the perspective that must be developed in staff if an effective marketing culture is to be established.

Never letting the client down

Do not promise what you cannot deliver and make sure that you deliver what you promise! Parents do not expect miracles but they do expect consistent, good quality education and, above all, that the school should honour its promises. If it promises to respond to parents' letters within two days, then it should honour that obligation. If a primary school promises to listen to children reading individually at least every day or if a secondary school promises homework on a Tuesday night, then the school has failed a performance indicator which it set itself if these activities do not take place. Performance indicators which a school sets for itself are the ones that, if broken, do the most damage to its reputation. Similarly, pupils who are promised visits that do not take place or hand in work for marking which is not returned on time (or even not marked at all) will have a broken promise and may develop negative attitudes.

There have been instances in which parents have attended parents' meetings and been told that the teacher does not like any children to get too far ahead in their work. This implies that the teacher is unable to cater for the needs of the individuals in a class. Parents will soon pass such messages on to their friends and acquaintances and the school will develop a poor reputation.

All these activities emphasise two points:

- the importance of clients in the eyes of the providers – if they have low priority or esteem they will be let down because it is not felt to be important to keep promises;
- the need to develop a strong consensus in the clients' collective opinion of the effectiveness of the school.

One impression of the school or many?

It is often said that 'first impressions count' and that the first impression which a client has of a school – for example the entrance hall or a friendly greeting from the school secretary – is critical. This is undoubtedly true but, from another perspective, clients make up their view of a school through a series of factors which, although individually insignificant, aggregate to give a very powerful message about the school. Such factors could be the quality of the newsletter, the telephone manner of the staff, the length of time it takes to respond to a letter or the quality of the organisation of the parents' meeting. All are contact points which either portray competence and care or incompetence and indifference. It is sometimes hard to convince staff that an activity such as offering a parent a cup of tea at a meeting can be critical in developing an opinion about the school. Such factors are very trivial in themselves but, when aggregated, they can form a chain of impressions about an individual member of staff or the school.

The message for schools is that all staff should be aware that every exchange with clients, no matter how insignificant it may seem at the time, may be critical in the chain of events which forms a client's opinion of an institution.

Ensuring that the school provides a service as well as a product

One of the great traditions of education in the UK is that it has always been regarded by its proponents at national and local level as an education *service*. We are not just in the business of providing a one-dimensional product such as test or examination results but a much broader approach which educates the whole person. If this is the case, we should focus much more on that service and how it is perceived rather than just on the product. For example, when teaching a particular lesson, the teacher is not just in the information transfer business, teaching the material and then going away. What he or she is involved in is a much more sophisticated and complex relationship with the child which focuses on other aspects of the child's development. The successful teacher shows that he or she recognises the individuality of the class members and values that individuality. It is aspects of the hidden curriculum such as caring relationships, encouragement and equality of opportunity which are important in developing the whole child. These factors and attitudes also give positive messages to parents about the school's approach to children. Staff, therefore, have to recognise and internalise these values not just because they are sound educational practice but because this 'service' element is a critical performance indicator for the school from the client's perspective.

Another example of this product-orientation which neglects the wider service aspects is provided by staff who become obsessed with activities such as form filling, routine marking, assessment and reports, neglecting the key role in a people-orientated activity – relating to their clients. Such routines should never be allowed to become purely administrative and mechanistic chores. The feedback which a pupil receives on a piece of work or a term's or a year's work should be part of the process of development and improvement. Clients expect useful feedback and the priority that is given to this aspect demonstrates the values and approaches of the school.

The management of a high quality service approach

A management priority in all organisations should be to adopt a client-orientation, focusing on the development of a high quality service approach. However, this is particularly difficult to achieve in an educational context for four reasons and these factors should receive significant management attention.

- When the educational product or service is being delivered to the client, whether it is a lesson for a child in the classroom or a conversation with a parent at a parents' meeting, the interaction is outside the direct control of the school's management.
- Once the educational service has been delivered there is very little that is tangible. The way in which an interaction is perceived determines how the quality of the school will be recognised. Thus the clients will *perceive* that they have (or have not) received a quality service in terms of a good lesson or a successful interview. This transitory interaction is, therefore, highly significant in assessing quality from a client's perspective. The significance of such interactions needs to be reinforced within the school.
- Although it is important to assess the quality of the whole educational experience, it is difficult for school leaders to monitor attitudes; attention has focused in the past on monitoring and evaluating educational processes. The ways in which staff are perceived and the pupils' views of the school have not traditionally received the same level of attention as these educational processes. A good example of the way that perceptions can be investigated is provided by the Client Attitude Survey questionnaire which is discussed in Chapter Eight and reproduced as Appendix 2. Schools should always take seriously the clients' perceptions of the product and service.
- There are many personnel with whom clients may come into contact. Wherever possible, clients should deal with as few people as possible. They should be able to identify and relate to key individuals and not be passed around the organisation from person to person. They can then form strong positive relationships with the key person who represents the school to them.

So how do we manage this high quality service approach? The key to success in this is defining standards and ways of dealing with clients that are developed and agreed by staff so that they feel they have 'ownership' of the concepts. Time will be needed for this policy development process. Time is also needed in order to undertake the necessary staff development so that all are aware of how to adopt a high quality service approach. There must also be a management framework to monitor the quality of the delivery of the product and service. Many schools have experimented with 'pupil tracking' as a monitoring device. This involves following one pupil through a week to analyse the quality of the educational experience received. This approach can be extended to observe other types of interaction, for example with parents. There should also be a regular reappraisal of how communications work – for example how enquiries are dealt with – in order to ensure that the system does not defeat its intent.

Developing a client-based philosophy

It is necessary to challenge the whole way in which we traditionally perceive schools and to construct a new philosophy about how we think about them. A fundamental approach in response to this challenge to the existing perception of schools is to reconsider the way we think about clients by asking the question, 'What are the assets of the school?' The traditional answer in accounting terms would be the buildings, the classrooms, desks, chairs and equipment. In human relations terms the answer would be the staff because they undertake the educational process.

These have always been misconceptions; schools are not of much use to society if they have furniture and teachers but have no children to be taught. They then become a waste of society's resources. A more fundamental analysis would establish that all these assets, both human and physical, only facilitate the education process. The key ingredient is the pupils themselves. Within the school a similar perspective can exist. For example, a librarian may consider a 'good' library as one with tidy desks and chairs and neat rows of books which fill the shelves, whereas the most effective library may be the one where children are sitting everywhere reading and the books, therefore, are off the shelves being used. So it is with the schools themselves. They do not exist to provide neat tidy buildings or jobs for teachers; they exist for the children and for their education. This has been brought into sharp relief in the UK with the advent of formula-based funding associated with Local Management of Schools and Grant-maintained Status. According to this new framework, empty chairs and desks are liabilities rather than assets. Rooms still have to be insured, cleaned, heated and other fixed costs met despite there being fewer pupils in the class. The real assets are the pupils and the parents who send them to the school. Without the pupils nothing else is possible; all the other components only facilitate the education process once this vital asset is in place.

This is a different, but necessary, way of thinking about the assets of the school. Organisations such as local government and the civil service have often been pilloried for being bureaucratic and more concerned with rules and regulations rather than with the people whom they serve. The structures and ways of working are not an end in themselves but merely a means of achieving a quality of service to a client. So it is in schools: all the buildings, organisational structures and staff only exist to provide the client with quality education. We should not, therefore, lose sight of this when organising the resources which deliver education.

Schools must stop being inward-looking and dealing only with the day-to-day problems and the challenges of the teaching process. They must consider the fundamental importance of the client in the school and how the recipients of education, their parents and the wider community, view the school. School leaders need to encourage this development of attitudes about the centrality of the client and to create significant management opportunities for promoting this way of thinking.

Creating a pro-active staff

This remains one of the major challenges in schools. Teachers are by definition concerned primarily with teaching children. While there has always been an accountability dimension to schools in that there has always been a need to communicate what they are doing and the quality of the process, this has been given increased importance by two factors:

- the establishment of frameworks to judge school performance in terms of the national curriculum and standardised assessment; and
- the operation of pupil number-led formula funding linked to open enrolment.

As we have mentioned before, to a certain extent educationalists have let others dictate the educational agenda because of their own reticence. How can leaders and managers in schools develop characteristics in staff to make them more pro-active in articulating the school's vision, values and achievements? Crego and Schiffrin in their book, *Customer Centred Reengineering* (1995) list what they call the 'Seven Cs' as a way of effecting the reengineering type of change that would be necessary in schools to create a more pro-active staff . These are:

- *Closeness* – to all customers, external, internal and stakeholders.
- *Clarity* – of vision and strategy.
- *Courage* – to make the difficult decisions and act.
- *Creativity* – to think outside the box.
- *Competencies* – which are distinctive, differentiating, and continually developing.
- *Commitment* – the will to persevere.
- *Consistency* – in words and deeds.

(Crego and Schiffrin, 1995, p78)

How then do we ensure that staff develop these characteristics, so that they can focus on the clarity of vision and purpose and also develop the commitment to express the vision at appropriate opportunities? One central role is to use staff development time not only to develop curriculum expertise but also to develop corporate vision and the interpersonal skills necessary to communicate the vision.

Conclusion

We have suggested in this chapter that to create strategic marketing intent it is necessary to create a strategic cause, to create a client-focused culture and to create a pro-active staff. We see this creation of a strategic intent as the vital first phase without which the effectiveness of the other two phases of our model (strategic market analysis and marketing implementation) will be seriously endangered. Having established this first phase we can now move on to Part Three of the book which considers, the process of strategic analysis of the educational market.

References

Bennis, W. and Nanus, B. (1985) *Leaders: The Strategies for Taking Charge*, New York, Harper and Row.

Crego, E. T. and Schiffrin, P. D. (1995) *Customer Centred Reengineering*, New York, Irwin.

Fullan, M. (1993) *Change Forces*, London, Falmer Press.

Jenkins, H. (1991) *Getting it Right*, Oxford, Blackwell.

Kawasaki, G. (1995) *How to Drive your Competition Crazy*, New York, Hyperion.

PART THREE

■ ■ ■

Strategic Market Analysis

4 **The Market Research Process** *41*

5 **Analysing the Environment** *50*

6 **Analysing the Competitors** *57*

7 **Analysing the Clients** *76*

8 **Analysing the School** *99*

9 **Integrating and Interpreting the Marketing Evidence** *118*

4

■ ■ ■

The Market Research Process

First find the information then make the decision

Introduction

This chapter outlines the principles of the market research process – the process which underpins the gathering of information in a school's strategic market analysis. The market research process is then applied in Chapters Five to Eight which examine in more detail the areas of information to be collected. Chapter Nine goes on to describe the process by which the information gained can be integrated and interpreted.

Market research is the systematic collection and analysis of information which relates to the school and the environment in which it is operating. It provides a means of qualifying and quantifying the nature of client wants and needs and of monitoring the school's effectiveness in satisfying those wants and needs. Information is gathered from both internal and external sources. It should be balanced, unbiased and provide a critical commentary on the current situation.

This awareness is necessary in the marketing process because it is neither desirable nor effective for those in a school to base their decisions about client wants and needs on personal assumptions. Nor is it desirable to make assumptions about the suitability of the present educational product or service, based on personal opinions. Such assumptions can be inaccurate and misleading; what is needed is accurate and objective information. Through the process of market research schools can collect factual data about the educational environment, the clients and about the school as it is currently perceived. Market research, therefore, comes early in the marketing process because it provides the information on which all subsequent decisions and activities are based.

This chapter examines why and when schools should undertake market research and who should carry out the market research. It then goes on to look at the stages in the process of market research.

Why should schools undertake market research?

A school carries out market research in order to acquire up-to-date information on which to base its decision-making regarding strategies for development and for effective interaction with its clients. In an open enrolment environment it undertakes this both to provide information which is vital at one level for survival and at another level for expansion and also to fulfil its accountability responsibilities more accurately and completely. Market research should therefore supply information which forms the basis for decision-making about the nature and quality of the product and service to be provided and about effective and efficient strategies for marketing that product and service.

The process of market research should enable the school to obtain specific information about the following four broad areas: the school's environment, the school's competitors, the school's clients, the quality of the school's product and service (*see* Fig 2.4, p20). Some of these areas relate to the external environment and some to the internal environment within the school. The nature of clients (as discussed in Chapter Seven) means that this area spans both the internal and external domains.

These are similar areas to those used in strategic/development planning so schools should not replicate their data gathering, but should make multiple use of the data available. The techniques which can be used to analyse each of these areas are discussed in Chapters Five to Eight.

When should schools carry out market research?

Market research follows on from the process of creating strategic intent. Once the vision and commitment have been established, information on which to base decisions has to be obtained to provide the focus for the marketing implementation stage. However, this need not be seen as a daunting task which takes place at a fixed point in every school year. There may be occasions when there needs to be a major focus on market research – for example, if there has been none carried out in the past or if it is felt that major changes in the external environment may not have been fully assessed by the school. Similarly, if major innovations or changes are planned it is important to assess the potential response of the clients and the competitors to those changes.

At other times, the school should use market research as an ongoing forecasting and monitoring device which takes place alongside other activities. It is important to spot trends and problems rather than waiting for things to go wrong or waiting until opportunities have been missed, hence the need for a regular market research process. Many market research opportunities exist and it is important to use the normal pattern of school activities to feed into this process – for example, through information gathered at events such as family assemblies, parents' meetings, open days/evenings and careers conventions. All staff can be debriefed after a parents' evening when not only the overt reactions to pupils' progress but also the covert information given to individual members of staff as asides could be aggregated to form a picture of underlying or developing concerns. These events can also be followed up by contacting a representative sample of those attending in order to gather information about their perceptions of the events themselves.

Who should carry out market research?

Each school will have to work out its own way of determining who will undertake the market research. The following questions should be addressed:

- Who will collect and analyse the information? Will this be left to individuals or a team of people? How senior will they be? Will such a team be limited to school staff or should it extend to include parents, governors, pupils and the wider community?
- Should the school buy in expertise? How would the cost of this relate to the cost of using internal staff, governors or parents? How long would it take 'outsiders' to understand the context, to win confidence and to gain access to informal information?
- Will interim progress reports be required? To whom will the researchers report back? What are the powers and responsibilities of the team undertaking the market research?

Internal staff have advantages in that they know the school's culture and many of the clients. They will also benefit from developing a wider perspective of the school's situation and will find the resulting data more acceptable because they have 'ownership' of it. They will develop a more critical awareness of the school and their role. On the 'down' side, they may lack objectivity and may be drawn away from important roles. A clear set of guidelines and clear proforma can help to overcome some of these difficulties.

It is necessary to clarify the issues outlined above before starting the market research activity, otherwise confusion about roles and responsibilities will ensue.

Steps in the process of market research

Just as it is important not to launch into the marketing implementation phase without first creating a strategic intent and carrying out strategic marketing analysis, so it is equally important that this strategic market analysis should not begin without careful preparation. Before rushing on, those responsible must consider the process involved and then work systematically through that process. This avoids starting at the mid-point with a number of misapprehensions and then having to backtrack. For example, it is important to determine the precise data required so that the school's leaders will be supplied with adequate information to make effective decisions while, on the other hand, avoiding the gathering of excessive amounts of data. The market research process can be divided into the four steps outlined below.

Step 1 Identifying information needs

Step 2 Planning the market research activity

Step 3 Collecting and analysing market research information

Step 4 Reporting the results of market research

Step 1 Identifying information needs

The senior management in a school should have a clear view about the types of decisions that are to be made, so that they can identify the information which must be acquired through market research in order to make those decisions. The decisions will fall into one of two groups: concerning either the *strategic context* in which the school operates, or the more *specific situations* or problems at the tactical level.

Strategic decisions will require information both on the broad educational environment and trends concerning the competitors, the client needs and expectations, the product and capabilities of the school. An example of this change in the strategic context would be the impact on parental opinion and on subsequent recruitment trends of a neighbouring school changing its age range.

As well as strategic marketing questions, there may be some specific issues which have arisen from previous research into broad areas or from a reactive response to a problem that the school is experiencing. Each fairly narrow problem must be identified and clarified before the market research process begins. For example, a school would seek opinions from parents in a very specific way about possible changes in school uniform policy and uniform design.

This stage – the establishment of a clear view of the school's precise problem or need for information – will help to focus the market research and save time and resources. The following example demonstrates the importance of this focusing down of the market research effort in order to clarify the precise nature of the investigation.

Decisions may be required within the broad area of home–school links but, before any market research begins, it is important to have a clear focus on the individual elements of that area. A school may feel that low attendance at parents' meetings is caused by the rushed interviews with individual teachers and so it may ask parents specific questions about this. In fact, the problem might be the timing of the events in the school year or the poor communication about their purpose. In either case, it would be pointless looking for ways of reorganising the appointment system. The danger is that, if the initial focus of the investigation is inadequate, the school can expend a great deal of time and effort to little avail.

Step 2 Planning the market research activity

Having identified the decision area and the information needed, it is then necessary to determine how that information might be gathered and analysed. For this to be done effectively, a structured approach is required. The school must go through a number of key questions concerning the framework within which the market research must operate. These questions will focus on:

- the sources of the information;
- the approaches to be used to obtain the information;
- the resources available.

Information sources

The key to success in effective market research is in assessing potential sources of information. These may be primary or secondary sources. *Primary information* is information gathered specifically for the task in hand. *Secondary information*, on the other hand, is so called because it is already available somewhere, having previously been collected for another purpose. No matter how the information is obtained, it should be evaluated to check that it is relevant, accurate, up-to-date and impartial.

Secondary information

This type of information is already in existence, either within the school or in the external environment. Researchers usually start by examining this because it can be obtained relatively quickly and cheaply. The researcher has to search through and sort material in existence rather than collecting new data. For example, data about each child (such as ability, medical conditions, address and travelling distance to the school) may be kept on individual files but would not always have been aggregated in a useful way. Useful secondary sources include:

1. *Internal information*. There is a wealth of *internal information* in the form of existing school documentation which can be utilised if it is re-sorted. Pupil attendance records, assessment profiles and staff records are examples of data that are collected for a specific purpose but which, when re-sorted and combined with other data, may provide valuable information to aid decision-making in a different management area. A simple analysis of the

postcodes of pupils coming to the school over the last five years will provide a pattern of information showing how the school has become more successful in recruiting in one area rather than another. A simple, but very significant, source is the pupils' work. If, for example, each pupil, during the first term after transfer to secondary school is asked to write an essay about his or her likes, dislikes, hopes and fears in the new school, then a wealth of information will be produced. It will be possible to see how the school is perceived, how that perception compares with reality and how successful the school has been in managing the transfer and creating a view in the pupils' and parents' eyes of a caring, effective school. Unfortunately, such information normally remains in the pupils' possession and is not used in a corporate manner.

There are many other examples of information that can be aggregated in a useful way to form a broader picture. Letters from parents and other clients which may be treated as isolated items can, if correlated, form an integrated picture. Inspection reports from OFSTED are another source of information waiting to be used.

2 *Central and local government information.* This would include national curriculum materials; assessment and testing regulations and guidance; Education Acts and circulars; LEA policy statements; local planning information, such as industrial and housing development proposals; regional statistics, for example on birth rate or unemployment. This type of documentation is the basis for much of the research into pupils' present and future needs, especially in an era of central determination of the curriculum. It also provides a lot of information on the local and national environment.

3 *Books, journals and the media* will give information about the environment in which the school currently operates, but they are also valuable in providing ideas and information for strategic direction, especially in relation to emerging technologies.

4 *Miscellaneous sources* could include: pressure group, press and publication releases; exhibitions, including other schools' open events; other schools' documentation; educational and other databanks; professional associations.

Although these sources may prove useful, there is a danger that excessive, unfocused information may be gathered from these wider areas. Care should therefore be taken to use them selectively. It may well be that secondary data cannot provide all the information that is needed. Often, more specialised information is needed. If this is the case, the school will have to undertake its own collection of original data from primary sources.

Primary information

This is information which is gathered specifically for the problem under investigation. A typical example would be a questionnaire to ascertain parental opinion on an issue. This type of information is likely to be more costly and time-consuming to acquire than secondary information because the researchers have to create the data as well as sort and interpret it. Before collecting primary data it will be necessary to consider the possible research approaches and to decide which will be used to obtain the data.

Research approaches

Depending on the information required, the choice will probably be between observation and survey methods.

1. *Observation research* involves observing relevant people, actions and situations. This is a useful method of collecting information that people are unwilling or unable to provide. Examples of such research would include:
   - telephoning the school to check the quality of response;
   - sending for a school brochure;
   - acting as a prospective parent;
   - tracking a pupil;
   - assessing ease of use of bus routes, parking and the buildings;
   - walking around the neighbourhood to assess general conditions and the environment.

   However, the observations, unless repeated several times, may not give an adequate sample on which to base major decisions although they do provide useful indicators for a more in-depth follow-up. The main drawbacks of this method are the time which may be required to carry it out and the fact that it may have to be carried out at a specific time.

2. *Survey research* can be considered to be the gathering of descriptive information. This is the most widely used method of determining people's knowledge, attitudes, preferences and choice patterns. Typically, this approach uses questionnaires and interviews and has either:
   - a structured approach – with formal lists and all the people being 'processed' in the same way; or
   - an unstructured approach – with the researcher probing and guiding according to response.

   One of the advantages of the survey approach is that it provides flexibility, making it possible for many kinds of information to be obtained in many different situations. It can be quicker than observational research. However, it has several disadvantages. People are sometimes unwilling to answer or have no time to respond. They may be tempted to give an answer even if they do not really know or they may be tempted to give an answer designed to please or deliberately to mislead. The method of contact used depends to a certain extent on the size of the research sample, on the research instrument and on resource constraints such as time, cost and opportunity for contact. Suitable methods include contact by mail, telephone or in person.

By using *postal questionnaires,* large amounts of data can be collected relatively cheaply. It is often thought that this method elicits more honest replies and eliminates interviewer bias. It does, however, require simple questions if standardised responses are to be obtained because it is not possible for the researcher to explain the questions to the respondent. The limitations of the method are that it takes time to receive the responses and often there is a poor response rate. It also has the limitation that the sender or recipient cannot develop answers from the predetermined structure and that anyone may complete the questionnaire and not necessarily the person for whom it was intended.

Contact by *telephone* ensures that the school can target the required individual. It has the advantages that it is quick and easy and the interviewer can explain the questions as necessary. It also allows the interviewer to develop the material and to respond to questions. There is usually a good response rate but there may be problems of cost, there is the possibility of bias in asking questions and recording answers and there could be sample bias if certain people do not have a telephone or are rarely at home.

Personal contact is a very effective way of obtaining information from individuals or groups. Using structured or unstructured interviews, this approach gives an in-depth opportunity to collect original data. The main disadvantages are the time taken (and therefore the cost) and interviewer bias. The advantages are that the interviewer can achieve a good response rate, knows that the right person is giving the responses and can develop points. This activity can be undertaken, for example, at parents' meetings or on industry liaison visits.

Resources

There will be inevitable resource implications when market research is being carried out. Staff will have to devote *time* to the exercise and some *materials* will be needed. Consideration must be given to the *quality* of the resources – for example, the skills which are available, whether or not the individual or team will require some training and, if so, where that might be available.

When the planning of market research is complete, the proposals should be approved by senior management before implementation. The aims and objectives should be clearly stated, along with the strategies for achieving these. Once they have given their approval to the market research approach, senior managers must be committed to resourcing that approach. They must determine the timespan of the exercise so that the results of the research can be fed into the decision-making process at the appropriate point.

Step 3 Collecting and analysing market research information

Once the first and second stages have been completed, the process of collecting and analysing the information can take place. Having defined the purpose, approach and tactics, the hard work begins. Often older pupils can undertake some collection and analysis as part of their studies as well as the marketing group undertaking its own activities.

Step 4 Reporting the results of market research

When interpreting and reporting findings, it is important to make sure that the report:

- is precise;
- is written in clear, simple language;
- gives a summary as well as detailed findings;
- is focused on the needs of the decision-makers;
- is focused on what can be achieved.

Conclusion

It can be seen from this chapter that market research or strategic market analysis is the second phase of the marketing process as shown in Fig 2.2. This research process involves analysing four main areas: the environment, the competitors, the clients and the school itself. These areas form the basis of the next four chapters and are followed by the final chapter in Part Three which considers how the evidence gained can be integrated and interpreted.

5

Analysing the Environment

Look at the forest, not at the trees

Introduction

The well-known maxim about 'not being able to see the wood for the trees' is especially relevant to planning and marketing in schools. There is a danger that schools react to immediate and local events and changes and do not pick out the wider trends which are often global and which will impact on the nature of schools and of learning. The learning business is rapidly changing so we need a process of analysing the environment that is not too rigid or detailed but which gives us a view of the dynamics of the world.

We reported in a research paper (Davies and Ellison, 1996) on the type of planning which is being undertaken in schools. We discussed the use of a three-stage process: 'futures' thinking; strategic planning; and school development planning. Our research showed that there is a lack of longer-term futures thinking and strategic planning in schools, compared with one- or two-year development planning. Schools are failing to analyse wider trends in the global environment. These trends are important not only for their current impact but also for their future impact on schools. For example, the increasing importance of technology or shifts in job security and work patterns are all part of the changes in the global economy that significantly affect schools. Similarly, at a national level, potential changes in government policy or in political control can have a radical effect on schools and need to be considered, if *ad hoc* reactive responses are to be avoided. The need for a 'futures' perspective is reinforced in the following extract:

> *A child starting school at the age of five in the year 2000 has a long educational journey to the completion of a university or a vocational education and will probably not start work until the year 2015 or later. That same child will be in the labour force in the year 2050 and beyond. What is more, that child could be working with*

technologies that have not yet been invented in an organisation that has yet to be created. (Davies, 1997, p12)

It is clear that one of the most important strategic roles for school leadership is 'managing the boundaries' – that is, seeing beyond the boundaries of the school and understanding the interface between the school and its environment. While leaders of schools must have an acute sense of the current environment, it is important that they challenge today's orthodoxy and envision and interpret what the future educational and societal framework will be. This is very significant from both a planning and a marketing perspective. As in industry and commerce, the planning and marketing functions are closely linked and the information which is gained through strategic analysis can be used in both processes. It will inform both what the school does in the future and how the school communicates that information through its marketing strategy.

How can the leader or manager break this information down and analyse its significance? This can be done by three levels of environmental scanning: global, national and local. The purpose of strategic analysis should therefore be to identify at each of the levels, trends which impact on the school and its context – for example, employment patterns, legislation, the effect of pressure groups, national politics, educational change. This is often referred to as a PEST (or STEP) analysis which considers **p**olitical/legal, **e**conomic, **s**ocio-cultural and **t**echnological factors.

The global environment

Several authors have written excellent books outlining the wider global trends or 'megatrends' and discuss their implications for education, employment, leisure and family life. These include Naisbitt (1982; 1995), Handy (1989), Naisbitt and Aburdene (1990) and Caldwell (1997). In the UK, the Technology Foresight initiative has looked at the future in a range of areas such as leisure and learning (Technology Foresight, 1995). Some examples of trends to consider are:

- the increasing importance of the Pacific Rim and Eastern European economies;
- the rapid transfer of information;
- the increased use of technology to perform a wide variety of tasks;
- the emergence of the virtual organisation;
- the increase in the number of jobs which one person will have in a lifetime and even at the same time;
- the changing role of women in society.

When the global trends are put together, there are significant implications for schools:

- The nature of work will be varied and will more often take the form of a service rather than a production function.
- The technology of learning will change.
- Data will be readily accessible.
- People will be brought closer together by communication systems.
- It seems probable that organisations which survive and prosper will be those which have flexibility and can respond rapidly to change.

It is worth spending some time considering the implications of these trends for the school so that plans can ensure that there is the flexibility and the capacity to be effective in the future. In order to analyse the environment at this level, a PEST analysis could be used to categorise the trends and to check that all areas have been covered.

Some of the trends which are impacting on schools are listed by Davies (1997, p20–21) and they can be categorised as follows:

Political/legal factors

- Significantly enhanced levels of consumer choice.
- The development of centralised curriculum and testing frameworks which provide measures of output and value-added, thus increasing information for parental choice.
- Increased differentiation between schools encouraging more specialised provision.
- Redefinition of the leadership and management functions in schools.

Economic factors

- Relating value-added educational gains to resource levels, allowing schools to be compared in terms of 'value for money' and forcing them to achieve increased performance with the same resource level.
- Considerable changes in staffing patterns and arrangements, involving more para-professionals, core and periphery staff, fixed-term performance-led contracts, school-site pay bargaining.
- Greater varieties of finance with blurring between state-only and private-only funding of schools.
- Contracting-out of educational as well as service elements of schooling.

Socio-cultural factors

- A re-examination of the boundaries between different stages of education and between education and the community.

Technological factors

- Radical changes in the nature of teaching and learning as the impact of the new teaching and learning technologies gathers pace.

The national environment

In order to analyse the environment at the macro or national level, a PEST analysis could again be used, highlighting the political/legal, economic, socio-cultural and technological trends that will affect schools and learning in the future.

When considering the *political/legal* developments which might impact on schools, it is important to try to predict the role of the public sector in the provision of education, UK and European policy and legislation regarding competition between schools, admission of pupils, funding mechanisms (such as vouchers and training credits), curriculum and assessment, staff pay and conditions, Health and Safety legislation. *Economic* factors to be taken into account in a strategic analysis include the state of employment and the economy, the nature of employment and industry and the impact of an ageing society on public expenditure. Under the *socio-cultural* category, the school should consider the changing role of women, the 'shrinking' of the world in terms of opportunities to communicate and to travel, an increasingly multi-cultural society, the concept of lifelong learning, the role of the home and family in the learning process. One of the most rapidly changing areas is that of *technological* development. It is important to gather information on the effect of technology on the transfer of information and the control of equipment, both in the community and, in particular within the learning technology.

Sources of information in this area could be a wide variety of government statistics and economic forecasts, the national press, the political parties' agendas and reports such as *Social Trends* (Central Statistical Office, 1994).

The local environment

There are many factors, often interconnected, in the local or regional environment which will impact on a school and its development. These will include:

- major regional initiatives such as industrial regeneration projects;
- local trends in employment;
- demography;
- housing and transport plans;
- local government policies and the impact of national government at the local level;
- other providers of education in the area (*see* Chapter Six);
- local community needs and client expectations;
- the changing nature of educational options in all phases.

There are many sources of information which are held locally or regionally but which are not usually drawn on by schools. A good example of the impact of a strategic change in the local environment was the opening of the new university in Lincoln in the autumn of 1996. This provided a focus for industrial regeneration, increased local employment, made a significant impact on housing and transport and was a focus for school-based educational development.

Undertaking the environmental analysis

The key shift in management is to develop a culture in the school which is outward-looking, client-focused and responsive to change. Staff, taking the lead from the senior management in the school, need to direct some of their in-service or professional development time to discussing broader strategic issues as well as current operational ones. The awareness of the need to scan educational developments on an international and national basis is as important as the mechanics of reporting the trends once they have been identified (*see* Exercise 5.1).

The PEST approach is a useful starting point and can be applied to each of the three levels of environmental analysis. Equally important is nominating individual staff with the responsibility for analysing information globally, nationally and locally. Increases or decreases in local employment rates or changes in local political control are often signalled in advance and scenarios can be developed by the school to cope with the changes. Similarly, the latest developments in the Internet where teachers can now download teaching material from a wide range of schools internationally does suggest that the wider educational environment is going to become a more important resource than the traditional teachers' centre.

Conclusion

This chapter has put forward the view that it is necessary to consider the wider environment in which the school operates as well as a detailed analysis of the competitors, the clients and the school itself. This environmental tracking has become even more vital with the increasingly rapid pace of change and the globalisation of economies and information systems. Having set up this broader environmental analysis, Chapter Six moves on to the analysis of the school's competitors.

References

Caldwell, B. J. (1997) 'Global educational trends and the expectations for the further reform of schools' in Davies, B. and Ellison, L. (eds) *School Leadership for the 21st Century*, London, Routledge.

Central Statistical Office (1994) *Social Trends 24*, London, HMSO.

Davies, B. (1997) 'Rethinking the educational context – a re-engineering approach' in Davies, B. and Ellison, L. (eds) *School Leadership for the 21st Century*, London, Routledge.

Davies, B. and Ellison, L. (1996) 'Building a futures and a strategic perspective in school development planning'. Paper presented at the BEMAS Research Conference, Cambridge, 25–27 Mar.

Handy, C. (1989) *The Age of Unreason*, London, Arrow Books.

Naisbitt, J. (1982) *Megatrends*, London, Futura Press.

Naisbitt, J. (1995) *Megatrends Asia*, London, Nicholas Brealey.

Naisbitt, J. and Aburdene, P. (1990) *Megatrends 2000*, London, Pan Books.

Technology Foresight (1995) *Progress Through Partnership: 14 Leisure and Learning*, Office of Science and Technology, London, HMSO.

Exercise 5.1 A PEST analysis of the environment

Complete the analysis chart below to indicate the most significant changes which are taking place in your school's environment.

	Global	National	Local
Political/legal			
Economic			
Socio-cultural			
Technological			

6

Analysing the Competitors

Second place is first loser

Introduction

Every school has a reputation and that reputation has to be managed. If you fail to manage your school's reputation, then competitors will soon start to take over your market. The market situation is a fast-moving one so it is important for school leaders always to keep an eye open to identify the competitors and their provision.

The concepts of school choice and open enrolment have increased parents' and pupils' ability to choose a school other than the one in the immediate area. Individual schools have been able to carve out a niche in the market so that parents have a range from which to choose. In the early years of schooling this has been facilitated by the introduction of vouchers for nursery places. At the secondary level, the opportunity to become a Technology or Language College has provided the potential for differentiation. The diversification of provision also allows for entry into the market of those who can offer education in a different form, either as an alternative to the traditional school or as a component of it. In the future, alternative forms of education such as home-based technology provision may be considered as competitors of the traditional schools. The competition, therefore, comes not only from a school down the road offering a similar product but, rather, from a range of providers, both existing and new, who are positioning their products according to both pupil needs and parental wants. Schools must identify the sources of pressure on them and identify the different groups of competitors. They must ask:

- Who are the school's major competitors now?
- Who (or what) is likely to be a major competitor in the future?

Having identified the competitors or potential competitors and examined their products and services, it is useful to consider the appropriateness of incorporating any of the new ideas into your own school's development.

Competitive forces

Writers on strategic management refer to the need to understand the competitive forces which impact on an organisation. In particular, Porter (1980) points out that the power of competition affects different providers in different ways. It is therefore important to gather your own information and not just to rely on the perceptions and responses of other schools or colleagues. Using the ideas of Porter (1980) and Bowman and Asch (1987), we have developed and applied the model for analysing a school's competitors illustrated in Fig 6.1.

It is important to identify the possible individuals or organisations at each of the points in the model so that a strategy can be developed which avoids threats and builds on opportunities. Exercise 6.1 at the end of this chapter is concerned with this identification process.

This chapter will focus mainly on the competitors that pose a threat and on suppliers. The power of users is only dealt with briefly as it will be the main focus of Chapter Seven which examines the school's clients, both internal and external.

The competitors

Existing providers

Most of the existing provision is by other schools in the locality although, for some more specialised schools such as grammar, boarding or special schools, parents will often be prepared to consider a wider geographical area. These existing providers exert power in the form of rivalry. It is important to monitor the activities, successes and failures of these other schools as they will be the first alternative for those clients in the area who are unhappy with your own provision. It is also useful to monitor the provision of schools in other parts of the country and overseas because, although they may not be direct competitors, ideas can be gathered about the way that products and services are being developed and the ways that schools are communicating with their publics.

When analysing other schools, you should consider both the type of provision which they offer and the quality of that provision. It is interesting to note that perceptions of these providers can be as important as the reality of what they are offering. As with your own school, the analysis should cover both the formal curriculum and the wider activities of the school as well as its styles of operation. It may be factors such as after-school activities and supervision which give them the competitive advantage. Staff in one of our research schools in the South of England investigated the reasons why parents were choosing a nearby independent school in preference to their own school and

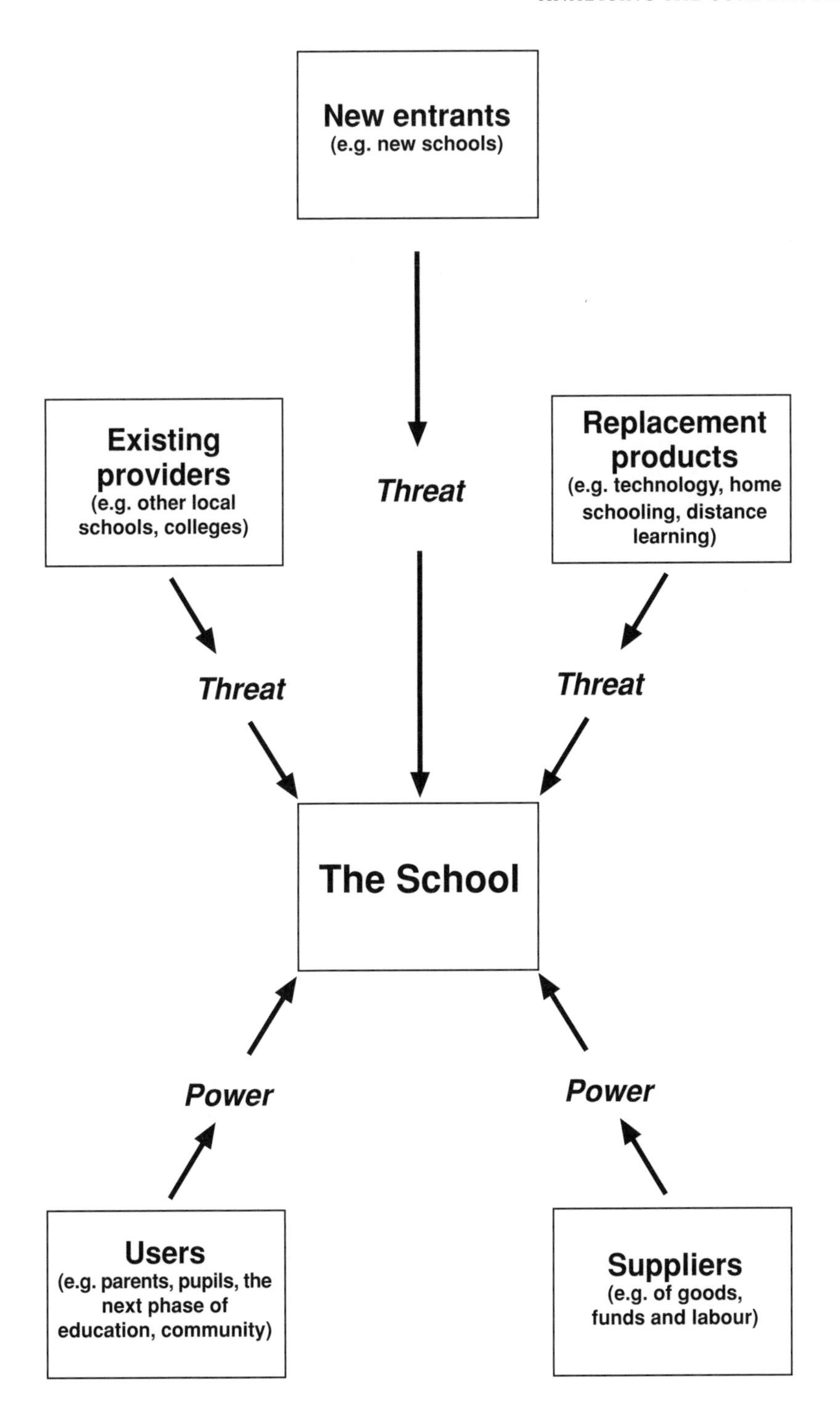

Fig 6.1 Competitive forces on the school

found that one of the significant factors was the existence of an extensive programme of Saturday morning sport. Needless to say, they then focused on re-introducing this in their own school. Even if such out-of-school provision were to mean a cost to the school or the parents, the income from extra pupils may compensate significantly for this. Competitor analysis of this kind has been carried out informally in some schools for many years but has had much more significance recently because of the competition for pupils who provide the main source of income. Exercises 6.2 and 6.3 at the end of this chapter focus on analysing the work of the existing providers.

The degree of threat from existing providers varies according to a range of factors. Some are the more obvious local ones such as distance to the nearest alternative, the quality of its product, its entrance policies and its marketing strategy. The work of Bowman and Asch (1987) can be adapted in order to analyse other factors which affect the degree of threat from existing competitors within an educational market. Some of the key factors which emerge are:

- *High fixed costs increase the desire to fill to capacity.* Chapter One explained the relationship between pupil enrolment, formula funding and school costs. In most cases the fixed cost element of a school budget is relatively high, at least in the short term, because even such variable costs as staffing cannot easily and quickly be adjusted if rolls change. Schools are now looking at the numbers in each year group and are seeking to improve their cost-effectiveness by ensuring a full intake. Those schools which are quite successful but not full should therefore merit particular attention.
- *A slow growth market means that most growth will come by taking pupils from the competitors' share.* This poses ethical difficulties for schools who are unhappy about being seen as trying to attract away other schools' pupils. Many areas have local informal agreements about the distribution of publicity materials but each school needs to keep an eye on the situation. Furthermore, private schools do not enter into such arrangements so that, while the state schools are operating an agreement, the private schools can take pupils from all of them. Even in areas where the agreement between the schools holds, parents will be exercising their rights. In one of our research areas, the two main secondary schools agreed not to distribute publicity material in each other's traditional catchment areas. This annoyed the parents who then had to use their own networks and resources to gather information about open evenings, activity days and so on. Another common problem in a slow growth market is that schools concentrate a lot of energy on trying to locate a few new pupils, perhaps from outside the traditional catchment area, while neglecting the product and service which is being offered to the current pupils/clients, who may then go elsewhere.
- *Large numbers of equally balanced competitors result in a complex market situation.* If a school makes small but significant changes to its provision or service, this may go unnoticed by competitors yet it can have a significant

effect on the balance of pupil numbers. Furthermore, in a closely competitive environment, there tends to be a high emphasis on publicity materials and wider factors related to new developments so that, here again, the quality of the product and service may be overlooked.

- *Lack of differentiation makes it easier to change from one provider to another.* In the school context, the national curriculum has provided greater consistency in terms of curriculum and expectations across schools. In the past, primary pupils who changed schools found themselves repeating a lot of topics and, at the secondary level, a totally different teaching scheme or range of options could cause considerable difficulty. Many schools are choosing to develop differentiated products, or unique selling points, such as nursery provision, after-school care, Language or Technology College status so that they can be attractive at the point of initial selection but this specialisation has the added attraction of helping to retain pupils who have no similar alternative in the area. Nevertheless, most children do not leave part way through a school unless they are moving away from the area or are very unhappy with the provision.

One way of gathering information on competitors is to follow up the parents who did not select your school to find out why they chose the alternative. This may sound difficult and you may feel that people, having made their choice, would not bother to supply this information. We have carried out a research project in order to investigate this problem for a group of schools and found that parents were very willing to give detailed reasons for their decisions and, in some cases, provided us with column-by-column comparisons on a range of criteria which they had used. Similarly, the views of prospective parents would be helpful in order to see how they perceive the competitors.

New entrants

New entrants to a market are defined as providers of a similar product and service. They may be completely new organisations – for example, a new school – or they may be formed when an existing school enters a new market through strategic development – for example, where a school has decided to extend its age range or when a comprehensive school begins to select pupils on the basis of ability.

When analysing the potential for new providers to enter the market, and hence the degree of threat to your own school, it can be helpful to view the situation from the perspective of the potential new entrant by considering the barriers which it would face as it tried to break into the market. These barriers fall into two categories: the reaction which such an entrant could expect from the existing schools; and factors relating to the general situation, especially those related to costs and the client base.

The competitive reaction of existing schools

New entrants may find it difficult to become established in an area if the existing providers are collaborating closely and resisting new entrants. Other adverse situations for new providers would be if the existing providers have the resources to retaliate or if the market is growing slowly so that existing schools are forced to take action against the new entrant. Before dismissing new entrants as 'no threat to the school', however, it is important to remember that new entrants may have modern facilities or offer other advantages such as continuity (as when extending the age range). These can be seen by the users (pupils) as opportunities and there may be a very positive attitude to them. This attitude will probably extend across a wide potential catchment area as a new entrant will attract considerable publicity.

Factors relating to the general situation

The questions below and in Exercise 6.4 will assist in analysing factors relating to the general situation which may affect the significance of any potential threat from new entrants.

- *Would there be high start-up costs, for example to meet capital requirements?* The need to provide new buildings or expensive equipment would deter new entrants unless there were government grants or private sponsors (as was the case with City Technology Colleges).
- *Could economies of scale be obtained in order to be cost effective?* For example, if a school wished to develop post-16 provision in an area with many other successful providers for this age range, it may find group sizes to be uneconomical.
- *Are there other favourable costing factors, such as location, skills, access to customers?* If a new school were to be opened, would it be possible to recruit talented staff? Is the district well served by public transport? If not, would parents be able to transport pupils to a new school?
- *Would it be possible to overcome customer loyalty to existing providers?* As discussed earlier, most pupils do not change schools part way through unless they or their parents are particularly unhappy with the provision. There are also 'traditional providers' in areas so that even new parents might be influenced to follow the norm. On the other hand, there is an attraction in the concept of something 'new', especially if the facilities are perceived to be of a high quality.
- *Are there high switching costs?* The cost of customers moving to the new supplier is usually only a minor issue in education (for example, a change of uniform).
- *What are the government's policies or possible policies which are relevant to the proposed market?* Cuts in public expenditure or a focus on work-based training could affect the expansion of the school sector.

Action should be planned to take account of any potential new entrants. Many commercial organisations have seen their products or services copied and taken no action at first, only to find later that the alternative is dominating the market.

Replacement products

One of the greatest threats to traditional schools over the next ten years will be the threat from providers of replacement products. These products may, in some cases, replace the use of the educational organisation as we know it – for example, with home schooling. In other cases, the products will replace part of the traditional schooling process – for example, where sixth formers spend part of the day working from home on distance learning packages – while the easiest situation to envisage is one in which the replacement products are integrated within the school, as in the case of integrated learning systems.

When analysing the threat from replacement products, it is important to take a very flexible and forward-looking approach and to keep the situation under constant review. An understanding of the global megatrends (discussed in Chapter Five) will help as will keeping an eye on developments in the electronics, consumer and leisure markets. The innovation sections of newspapers can give an indication of new technology which could affect the role of traditional educational organisations. The following factors will be of most significance.

- *The rapid developments in technology, especially the miniaturisation of equipment.*
- *The linking of people at different sites through communications technology.*
- *The increased frequency of job changes and more people working from home.* This will mean that learners will need updating through lifelong learning, and also that there may be adults at home during the day with equipment available which could also be used by those who are traditionally thought of as being of school age.
- *Concern for the environment.* This may affect the sustaining of school buildings which are only used for 14 per cent of the hours in a year. There may be pressure to reduce travel by motor vehicle and to cut down on the use of materials such as paper.
- *The economic climate.* It is unlikely that there will be any more money for education in most Western countries.
- *Teacher supply.* There may be a shortage of good teachers, particularly in certain specialisms, as is already apparent in parts of Australasia and the UK.
- *The employment situation.* There could be more emphasis by governments on on-the-job training. Even the plentiful supply of jobs in an area acts as replacement product for pupils of school-leaving age.

Many replacement products will be based on IT or text and will have the capacity to be used over a wide geographical area (including world-wide) and for a wide age range, thus achieving economies of scale and cost-effectiveness. It may be possible for consumers to switch partially to such products, thus avoiding any barriers of loyalty and risk.

Any analysis of the degree of threat from providers of replacement products would include a consideration of the questions listed in the previous section in relation to new entrants. Such an analysis (*see* Exercise 6.4) would probably show that many of the barriers would be much easier to overcome for those who are developing something 'different' and this should alert current providers to this particularly strong threat to their continued existence in their current form. It would be more difficult for existing organisations successfully to keep out providers of replacement products through close collaboration, especially products of a technological nature. They may, however, diversify in order to provide such products themselves.

Suppliers

The power of suppliers is a force to consider. Schools are very dependent on people as resources so it is appropriate here to consider them as well as the traditional suppliers of goods such as educational equipment or of services such as energy.

Suppliers can influence the way the product and service is developed, delivered and marketed by what they can offer and how much they charge. Changes in the power of the suppliers of goods have been especially noticeable since the Education Reform Act. There is now less of a monopoly use of one supplier in a district than was the case, for example, with the centralised supply of computer hardware by LEAs in the 1980s. On the other hand, there has been a rise in the number of schools who have obtained some form of sponsorship from a manufacturer or supplier, thus tying them, at least in the short to medium term, to a particular product or service. Suppliers can even set up rival businesses – for example, when the software and hardware suppliers diversify into integrated learning systems with support for use at home. If the concept of suppliers is extended to include the suppliers of funds, then here again, rival organisations can be set up or supported if the funders are unhappy with your provision. This can be seen quite clearly in the private sector, with special educational needs and even, through the actions of central government, in the closing of 'unsuccessful' schools and the opening of new ones.

Those who work in the school also exert power as suppliers of labour. If a school takes no account of this power, it may find that staff are unhappy with the hours of work, the conditions and opportunities, the teaching and learning process or the management and leadership style. Failure to obtain suitable staff will mean that a school is unable to provide effective education for its clients (the 'users' in Fig 6.1) and they will go elsewhere, threatening the survival of the school. Here too, the suppliers of labour can set up their own business such as a competing organisation.

Schools can begin to control the supply of goods and labour by the process of backward integration. They can train their own staff through School-centred Initial Teacher Training. They can produce their own workbooks and computer software. They can employ their own catering, cleaning and grounds maintenance staff rather than relying on contractors. In some areas schools have co-operated to overcome a problem in supply. For example, one school provides a relief caretaker service for a group of local schools because the original supplier of the service was affecting the quality of provision. In some cases, however, this diversification takes schools away from the core business of teaching and learning, especially in small schools.

Users

Users are traditionally seen as the pupils or students. It is important to consider the power of the parents of these children and of other learners who are attracted. Without the learners there is no school. Schools need to take into account, therefore, the degree of choice which these people have now and may have in the future about the location of learning and about the type of product offered. While they do exert power, especially through the open enrolment legislation, each person has a limited impact and is only in the school for a short period of time. Alternatively, the power of users can be seen in relation to those who ultimately benefit or receive the outputs of the education process – for example, the next phase of education, employers or the community. These are groups with a longer-term interest and a greater collective power.

Users tend to exert a strong force when:

- there are several providers in the area so they can obtain the product and service elsewhere;
- there are low costs in switching to another provider;
- they have the power of law behind them so that they can insist on changes to the product and service delivered or so that they can transfer;
- they are very dependent on the 'right' product in order to carry out their current or future role;
- they could manage without the product;
- they could opt for backward integration and produce the product themselves – for example when a secondary school sets up a primary section so that it does not rely on being a user of the output of the local primary schools.

Until recently, there has been a tradition of producer capture and a lack of consideration of the skills and knowledge which others expect schools to provide through the learning process. It is important that the strategic market analysis considers the needs of the users and their expectations of the school. This analysis of the factors which affect users is covered in Chapters Seven and Eight.

Conclusion

One of the most significant barriers to entry into an educational market is the existing organisations' long history of providing quality education. We would add to this the existing providers' effective communication of that quality to the appropriate client groups.

Is your area ripe for new providers and new products or to be controlled by the suppliers and users? Will you be put out of business by the other schools in the area? The exercises which follow will help you to analyse your competitors.

References

Bowman, C. and Asch, D. (1987) *Strategic Management*, Basingstoke, Macmillan.

Porter, M. (1980) *Competitive Strategy*, New York, Free Press.

Exercise 6.1 The competitive forces

Using the categories in Fig 6.1, list the organisations, individuals, groups or types of product which fit into each of the five classifications of competitive force as they impact on your own school.

Existing providers
New entrants
Replacement products
Suppliers
Users

Analysing the existing providers

In order to reduce time pressures, you should choose your significant rivals for detailed data collection. This requires that in Exercise 6.1 you have been careful about the listing, as a major rival may not be the nearest school or the one with the best results in the area.

The data collected should be both quantitative and qualitative data, although the latter requires more effort to be accurate. You should collect from a range of sources as this will assist with accuracy and you should keep updating the picture from a range of data sources.

Exercise 6.2 Monitoring quantitative data on the competitors

Assemble the data which can easily be quantified and which can be kept up to date as well as being relevant and cost-effective in terms of collection time, and record it in the chart on the next page. Published information is an obvious first source.

Quantifiable data for your school and its main competitors

	Total roll	*Roll of entry year*	*No. of first choice applicants*	*Key stage results*	*Exam results*	*Unit costs*	*Pupil/ teacher ratio*	*Unauthorised absences*	*Exclusions*
Your school									
School A									
School B									
School C									

Exercise 6.3 Gathering qualitative information about competitors

This is a more complex task than gathering numerical data and the sources of information will be very varied. The picture will build up over time although, here again, it will need to be kept up-to-date. It is inappropriate to provide a matrix for this information but we provide a set of key questions which should help in the research process.

1 What is the competitor trying to achieve? What is its purpose?

- What is its vision/mission statement?
- What are its goals/objectives?

These may be found in the prospectus, publicity material and other publicly available documents. In the case of a school, they will probably form part of the headteacher's speech on occasions such as an open day/evening.

2 What is the competitor doing to achieve its goals?

- What is the curriculum being offered? Is there a particular emphasis, for example on language, technology, able children, integration of children with special needs? Is there provision for vocational education?
- What are the arrangements for transition, for example primary–secondary links, school–post-compulsory links?
- What types of extra-curricular activities are available and when do these take place?
- Can the pupils be cared for beyond a traditional school day?

This information will be available through prospectuses, publicity materials, newsletters and the local press.

3 What resources and facilities are available?

- What is the expertise of the staff to deliver the curriculum which is offered?
- What is the rate of staff turnover? Are many jobs readvertised?
- Are there any redundancies/cutbacks which could affect morale?
- What is the standard of the facilities like, particularly in specialist areas such as technology, science, nursery/reception?
- Is there a swimming pool?
- Are any new facilities planned?
- Do learners need equipment at home?

Some of this information can be gleaned from the press, but much will be via the local grapevine. Governors and staff can be a good source of this kind of information.

4 How does the competitor communicate with its clients?

This is a significant area because, as discussed in Chapter One, it is no use having a good product but not letting anyone know about it. It may be that a competitor's product and service is quite comparable to your own in relation to the questions discussed above but that its competitive edge is gained by effective communication. This communication may well be reaching the clients in 'your' area and having an adverse effect on your own recruitment.

- How effectively and how frequently does the competitor use each of the following:
  - newsletters?
  - the local or national press (especially in relation to its 'unique selling points')?
  - open days/evenings?
  - networks of friends and neighbours?
  - family assemblies or social events such as concerts?
- How widely is the school communicating its advantages? Is it openly recruiting from the traditional catchment area of other schools? (Even if there is no direct effect on your school, there could be an indirect, 'knock-on' effect.)

5 How effective is the competitor?

It is important to know whether the competitor is providing quality education or whether all the media coverage is just 'hype'. This is a very difficult area because the most accessible information tends to be raw data such as examination and test results. OFSTED reports are available to all if a detailed analysis is needed. The local grapevine, such as parents and the local press, usually picks up on problems rather than strengths so this should not be taken as too reliable. Parental perceptions could be surveyed.

Exercise 6.4 Analysing the potential for new entrants and replacement products

As indicated on pages 62 and 64, a similar set of factors determines the degree of threat from both new entrants and from replacement products. Apply the questions below in either situation. The questions relate to the factors outlined on page 62 and cover the two categories: the reaction which such entrants could expect from the existing schools and factors relating to the general situation, especially those related to costs and the client base.

	Yes/No	**Notes**
Are the existing providers collaborating closely and resisting new entrants?		
Do the existing providers have the resources to retaliate?		
Is the market growing slowly so that existing schools are forced to take action against the new entrant?		
Are other providers offering the same combination of features?		
Would there be high start up costs, for example to meet capital requirements?		
Could economies of scale be obtained in order to be cost-effective?		
Are other costing factors favourable, for example location, skills, access to customers?		

	Yes/No	Notes
If new provision were to be opened, would it be possible to recruit talented staff?		
Is the district well served by public transport or would parents be able to transport pupils to the new provision (if necessary)?		
Would it be possible to overcome customer loyalty to existing providers?		
Are there high switching costs?		
Are there any government policies or possible policies which are relevant to the proposed market?		
Are there any cuts in public expenditure or a focus on a particular area that could affect the financial viability of the new entrant?		

Exercise 6.5 Examining the suppliers

Use these questions when considering the supply of goods, services and labour such as trained teachers. With some modification, they can be used to consider the school's funders/sponsors.

1 Who are the school's major suppliers?
2 Are these the major suppliers of these products and services to most schools?
3 Why are these suppliers used (e.g. quality, cost, ease of supply, service availability)?
4 What are the alternatives?
5 How much does each supplier influence the way in which the product or service is delivered?
6 Is this influence acceptable?

7 How can the power of suppliers be harnessed to the school's advantage:

(a) for marketing?

(b) for school development?

7

Analysing the Clients

If you don't know what they want, how can you give it to them?

Introduction

Chapter One considered the question 'To whom are schools marketing?' and showed that there is a wide range of clients for whom the school provides its products and services, either directly or indirectly. A considerable amount of information about the clients is needed in order to build up a picture which can inform the school's future direction and can help to determine its message and means of communication with those clients. Chapter One also discussed the overlapping use of the terms 'consumer', 'customer' and 'client'. For the sake of simplicity, we will refer here to all groups as 'clients' but will seek to identify the important features of each group so that a differentiated marketing approach can be developed. We will give guidance on identifying the following:

- the nature of the market segments;
- the wants of the clients;
- the needs of the clients;
- the behaviour and activities of the clients.

When analysing the clients, it is necessary to assess not only the current position but also to identify potential changes and trends that may alter that position and, thus, create new or alternative segments which can be exploited in the future. Any changes in wants, needs and behaviour should also be monitored. The exercises at the end of the chapter will provide a framework for analysis.

It is also important to understand the clients' perceptions of the product and service offered by your school and by the competitors. This area will be covered in Chapter Eight.

Market segments

Market segmentation has already been defined in Chapter One as a way of dividing clients into groups with similar needs. In order to examine the market for the school's product and service, determine the types of messages which need to be put across and consider where the key influences lie, it is important to divide the clients and the potential clients – a heterogeneous group which is both internal and external to the school – into more homogeneous segments. Using the categories first established in Chapter One, we can now describe some of the segments of a school's market and their key features. Exercise 7.1 allows you to consider the segments relevant to your school.

Internal markets

The individuals and groups within the internal market are those who know the school best. They are therefore in a position to be significant ambassadors for the school and to influence all clients' perceptions of it. It is most important that such influence is used to give positive messages about the school; these internal groups should understand the importance of having a client-focused culture (as discussed in Chapter Three). Exercise 7.2 asks you to consider the role of those people who constitute the internal market of your own school.

Governors

The governors need to play an active role in the management of the school if they are to understand the school and be committed to achieving its aims. Increasingly, governors are realising that they have a difficult and time-consuming task. They will only be able to play an effective and informed role in managing and marketing a school if they work in partnership not only with the senior management team, but also with the pupils and parents.

Staff (teaching and support)

As was explained in Chapters One and Three, it is important that these internal partners in the education process have a clear view of the aims of the school and the policies for achieving these aims. Senior management should help all staff to realise that they each have an important part to play in managing the school's reputation as they implement these policies and in their communications with those outside the school's traditional boundary.

Regular visitors and helpers

These people may only be in the school for a short time so it is especially important that they can recognise quickly that quality and commitment are being combined to give effective education for the pupils. It is all too easy for such visitors to leave with a biased, unfavourable view of a school based on an isolated incident. Care should be taken to ensure that they are given relevant and positive information to take with them to the external environment.

Current pupils

The current pupils are very significant now that so much of a school's funding is roll-related. Although they tend to stay throughout the school unless there are major problems, there are some key points when a transfer may be considered, in particular the points at which they change from one key stage to another. This is especially true where areas with middle schools border areas with transfer at the age of 11. In areas where pupils may go to independent schools, there are different key ages, depending on the type of school.

Current pupils can be key ambassadors because they carry both explicit and implicit messages about the school as they move around in the community. Through positive reinforcement they need to be made aware of the school's aims and its achievements so that they can communicate an effective message.

As well as acting on behalf of the school, the current pupils can provide data to inform the marketing process. Although individual information is kept on where each pupil lives, most schools do not then use this secondary data to collate records of their current recruitment area or to look at the recruitment area of their competitors. Exercise 7.3 suggests the use of a map to display the information but a database could also be used. This monitoring has been used successfully by one of our research schools to track recruitment patterns and is particularly effective when the recruitment area is large or when there are rapid changes in recruitment patterns. If appropriately structured, the investigation can form part of a pupil project or a research project for a higher education award.

This type of information gathering can be extended to include those pupils who would normally attend the school but are 'lost' to competitors.

Current parents

The parents of current pupils are a very important client group. It is obviously desirable to maintain their support so that these pupils remain in the school but it should not be forgotten that there may also be younger children to follow. Parents make a choice to send a child to the school. If they perceive that the child is receiving a 'good' education and if that fact is being communicated to them, then they will be satisfied with what they are receiving. Schools should ensure that parents have their original choice reaffirmed by effective positive communication about the school and about their child's progress.

Of equal importance is the fact that parents are very often the key influence-makers in the local community. They can act as excellent ambassadors for the school to the external market – that is, friends, colleagues and neighbours with children. On the other hand, while only a few parents are so dissatisfied with a school that they actually move their child to another school, they do express dissatisfaction to friends and neighbours locally who are then persuaded against choosing the school. This is the latent effect of parental influence, whether negative or positive; it may not be noticed immediately but may take two or three years to work through.

Bradley (1996) found evidence of the importance of the current parents. In his study, the knowledge of a school obtained through already having children at the school or from the parents of other current pupils were two of the top five most used and most useful sources of information for those choosing a secondary school. It is therefore important to ensure that current parents have a clear and positive view of the school, not only to develop their understanding of the product and service which they are receiving but, through them, to build the school's reputation and intake in the future.

External markets

The need to attract new clients, from both within and outside the traditional catchment area of the school, is one of the main reasons why many schools first begin to explore the concept of marketing. It is the attraction of new clients (pupils and parents) that ensures the continuing success of the school. Here also lies one of the major professional objections to the marketing of schools – the idea of 'poaching' pupils from fellow professionals. It is to be hoped that the approach to marketing which is outlined in this book – that is the management of a school's reputation through the communication of a 'quality' message – will help to counter these objections. Alongside the pupils and parents, there is a need to consider the wider external markets, both within and beyond the education system.

Prospective pupils

There is considerable awareness among pupils of the school choice issue and of the effectiveness debate, both of which receive so much attention in the media. Schools need to be aware of the numbers of prospective pupils in their potential market and of the current locations of those pupils in order to plan their school development opportunities as well as their marketing activities . It is useful to sub-divide prospective or potential pupils by gender, aptitude, current place of education and so on. This is especially so if a school is trying to differentiate its marketing strategy to reach and appeal to different groups of prospective pupils. Some schools wish to target specific groups – for example, to make up the numbers in a particular year group, to maintain a particular balance of pupils such as a comprehensive intake or to alter a perceived imbalance, such as an excess of boys in a coeducational school.

A primary school might identify the following groups of prospective pupils in order to focus its communication strategies effectively:

1 *For entry to the nursery*:
   - local children currently at playgroups;
   - local children not currently at playgroups;
   - those from beyond the traditional catchment area currently at playgroups;
   - those from beyond the traditional catchment area not currently at playgroups.
2 *For entry to the reception class*:
   - those currently in the school's nursery;
   - local children attending nursery school elsewhere;
   - local children not attending nursery school;
   - those from beyond the traditional catchment area not in the school's nursery.
3 *For entry at other points*:
   - those in the traditional catchment area currently going to another school;
   - those moving into the area.

One of our research schools, a Catholic upper school, investigated the prospective pupils and identified the following groups:

- Catholic pupils in the town approaching the age of transfer;
- Catholic pupils outside the town with parents willing to transport them;
- non-Catholic pupils, generally middle-class, seeking a place at the school because of its reputation;
- non-Catholic pupils, generally not middle-class, living near the school;
- current Year 11 pupils seeking an A-level course;
- current Year 11 pupils seeking vocational courses;
- Year 11 pupils elsewhere seeking a different place for sixth-form studies.

These particular schools must next determine the size of each group, consider whether or not the school feels that it wishes to encourage them to attend and then devise appropriate communication strategies.

Many enticements are offered to pupils to go to see their next school or to make a definite choice at different stages of their education. These enticements include: activity days; concerts and Christmas productions; open days; Christmas and summer fairs; free gifts and even, to those aged 16, financial incentives to enter certain forms of post-compulsory education. Schools need to consider the appropriateness and effectiveness (including cost-effectiveness) of the various means of communicating the school's product and service to the prospective pupils. This will require some consideration of the needs and perceptions of these clients and monitoring of the existing marketing activities of the school and its competitors.

Prospective parents

Parents are now aware of the existence of a choice mechanism, so schools must be ready to respond positively to requests from them for information or for visits to the school. Bradley (1996) shows that in the area which he researched, visits to the school were the most used and the most useful source of information to parents making a choice of school. Schools must ensure that these visits are carefully managed, remembering the advice in Chapter Three to 'never let the client down'. There are many tales on the grapevine (the next most used and useful source emerging in Bradley's study, after visits and personal experience) of parents not being shown round by the teacher that was expected to do this. This failure to keep a promise gives parents implicit messages about the relative importance of the potential pupil and family in relation to other tasks in the teacher's day. Most parents are shown round by a member of the senior management team or the person responsible for the intake year group and times are usually flexible to meet parents' needs. However, we have heard of parents being told at an information evening 'Please don't ask to be shown round before the Open Evening on 9th November'. Such parents may have chosen another school before then as suggested by Ries and Trout's statement that it is:

> *much easier to get into the mind first than to try to convince someone you have a better product than the one that did get there first.* (Ries and Trout, 1994, p3)

Former pupils

As with current pupils, those who have left the school have considerable knowledge of its strengths and weaknesses. They have very clear perceptions of the way in which they were valued and the quality of the teaching. It is important that these pupils leave with a positive image and that the school, wherever possible, continues to communicate with them, either individually or through the media. Many people have a nostalgic view of their time in a school, so they can be very positive ambassadors and, in some cases, can act as substantial financial benefactors. It is helpful if any reunions can be held on the school premises to give the opportunity to promote the school's current facilities and to promote its strengths.

Prospective staff

There are well documented cases of schools being unable to recruit either the quality or quantity of staff which is desirable, especially in certain subjects and geographical areas. It is therefore important to communicate a clear and positive picture of the school to prospective staff so that they apply for and accept posts which are offered.

One of the key dimensions here is whether or not the existing staff speak highly of the school when they talk to prospective colleagues. There may be a 'staffroom mafia' which provides a cynical view of the school to potential colleagues; if so, this needs to be countered. There are various factors which a school must address. What arrangements are made for advertising, interviewing and appointing staff? What are staffroom facilities like? How helpful are secretarial and support staff when prospective staff telephone the school? What coherent staff development policies are available so that staff can extend their skills and knowledge, and hence their effectiveness, in the future? Would staff recommend a colleague to work there? What messages do they give when they meet professional colleagues at meetings or conferences, especially in the bar afterwards? In an era of increasing staff shortage these factors can be critical in establishing a 'good reputation' for the school as an employer and retainer of staff.

Other educational institutions

Most of the pupils who enter any school will have been in some form of local organisation such as a playgroup or a feeder/partner school in the previous phase of education. The view of the schools in the next phase which is held by the parents, pupils and staff at the feeder school can be critical to the decisions which both parents and pupils make. All these clients should be convinced that there is true continuity and progression between the phases. In particular, the historical primary/secondary divide has to be broken down and reinterpreted as a total package of educational provision from the age of three to eighteen. People can only be convinced that this is so if the reality is reflected in the working relationships between the different partners in the education service. To date too many of the links have related to the pastoral care of pupils during the transition phase while the biggest source of discontinuity has remained in the approach to teaching and learning and in assessment, with the result that pupils' progress is often temporarily reversed.

A secondary school with a sixth form needs to relate to other secondary schools in order to market this provision to pupils who might transfer in at the age of 16. This will help to ensure the viability of its own provision but can be a very sensitive area, even with 11 to 16 schools, as they may have other partnerships – for example, with a sixth-form college or a tertiary college.

A school's reputation with further and higher education institutions is more complex. When considering places for school leavers, the range of possible destinations is so great that concentrating on a limited number with whom to forge close links may be the best strategy. If relationships are good, local universities can provide valuable services such as the use of facilities and support for teaching staff in the form of students on placement or guest lecturers. It is worth remembering that universities also need students. They will see secondary schools as clients and will be anxious to help and to build links.

The local community

Members of the local community contribute (through local and central government taxes) to the funding of state education. As many schools know to their cost, local reputations take a long time to build but are very quickly lost. It is important, therefore, to maintain a positive image within the community. However, the individuals within that community are very diverse and have different perceptions of what a school should be so that it is difficult to satisfy everyone. It is necessary to target key people with influence locally – such as councillors, the press and community leaders – and to ensure that they are kept informed of school developments and involved in appropriate activities.

There are often key points where the school comes into contact with the community such as outside the gates or on the buses which take pupils home after school. The behaviour of pupils here may be more critical in determining the school's reputation than more formal interactions. Key points such as this need careful monitoring.

Commerce and industry

For a variety of reasons, it is important to market the school to local businesses, to the local Training and Enterprise Council (TEC) and to associated liaison groups such as the Chamber of Commerce. Industry and commerce usually have a view of the quality of education in a school even if this is based on hearsay. Good relationships could enhance the promotional process because, when new employees move into the area, they will be told of a school's reputation and may choose it for their children.

The quality of relationships will affect the availability of jobs for pupils. In the future there may well be fewer jobs, especially for inexperienced school leavers, so strong links will enable the school to ensure that pupils meet the needs of the employers and that the employers are aware of this capability. An ever-increasing percentage of pupils are now taking part in work experience schemes and the availability of quality placements will depend on the employers' perceptions of the school (and of its pupils). Furthermore, if a school has marketed itself well and has a good reputation, then it will be much easier to have involvement with commerce and industry for careers advice, staff development and enterprise schemes.

Sponsorship (usually in the form of goods or services in kind) may well be available to those schools which best communicate the quality message. Local and national businesses have their own reputations to protect so it is unlikely that they will wish to be associated with badly managed schools which are not meeting the needs of the pupils.

The Local Education Authority/Funding Agency

For a maintained school, the Local Education Authority (LEA) or Funding Agency is an important stakeholder because it is providing funds so that the school can function. It is, therefore, a client of the school with the school undertaking to provide a number of places and educational provision on its behalf. In all dealings with such organisations, the school should present a competent, business-like image. This would include having well-thought out plans, making clear bids and, in the case of disputes, having an accurate record of any evidence or incidents.

The Office for Standards in Education (OFSTED)

Now that most schools have been through the initial four-yearly inspection from OFSTED, they hope to have minimal contact with such bodies as they move to a greater focus on the less successful schools! Nevertheless, the general messages which are put out by national government about types of schools, about standards or about particular approaches to teaching and learning have a profound effect on clients. Schools also need to track the messages which are being put out as there may be a need to take on certain ideas or to carry out a damage limitation exercise with parents or in the local press if the messages appear to reflect badly on the school. On the other hand, a satisfactory report from inspectors or a central government message which appears to support what the school is doing should receive maximum coverage.

As schools move to be more self-evaluating, there should be a clear marketing message – that a quality product is being delivered and that quality management is part of the everyday operation of the school.

The Teacher Training Agency/General Teaching Council

Schools, both collectively and individually, need to have good relationships with whatever organisations are responsible for the quality of the profession. This is a two-way process in that, as well as promoting a positive image, the schools must be prepared to listen to the messages of good practice coming from such organisations.

National groups and organisations

Since 1976, there has been an ongoing debate about educational standards in state schools. One way of counteracting the extensive coverage given to poor standards is to market the schools in a very positive way to central government, local Members of Parliament and, via the media, to the country as a whole.

Various specially funded projects take place in schools and care should be taken at all levels to ensure that such funding continues. The availability of specific grants and various types of sponsorship will depend on the providers' perceptions of the 'value for money' which results from the investment.

Future market segments

It is very important for strategic leaders to predict new market segments which will usually have some relationship to the ones listed above. Some creativity and knowledge of global trends is required in order to do this. For example, it may be important to consider wider funding agencies such as the European Union and a wider range of potential learners such as those from overseas. Countries with similar open enrolment and formula-funding policies, such as New Zealand, are already involved in marketing overseas as are some UK state schools and, of course, the boarding schools have been involved for many years.

The wants of the clients

All client groups have wants which are met by individual schools to a greater or lesser extent. As we explained in Chapter One, there is a lack of homogeneity among the clients and their wants, so it is not possible to match all of these to the school's product and service. It is, however, very important to be fully informed about what the clients expect from education in general and the school in particular. Schools must, therefore:

- identify clients' present wants – in terms of the nature and quality of the product and service; and
- identify the anticipated wants of the present clients and of the potential clients.

The school can then use this information when developing and promoting its product and service, always bearing in mind that the wants of parents or pupils reflect what they *perceive* that they want and do not always reflect the *actual* needs of these clients, especially the needs of the pupils.

One of the ways in which schools can monitor parental wants is to examine the reasons why parents and pupils choose schools. There have been many studies in the UK covering a variety of geographical areas and socio-economic groups. The information obtained can give an understanding of the reasons for selecting schools, provided that it is borne in mind that genuine reasons may not always be articulated by the clients. Research on middle-class choices in an inner London LEA (West, 1992) showed that middle-class parents with children of above average reading ability selected private schools because of good discipline, good examination results and because they felt that the school would suit their child's needs. West also found that such middle-class parents who chose schools in a different LEA did so because of their perceptions of discipline, good examination results and 'a pleasant atmosphere'. The most detailed research which we have seen is that obtained through the Open University's PASCI study (*see*, for example Glatter, Woods and Bagley, 1995).

This covers a range of types of school, socio-economic circumstances and areas, including rural, town and inner city and appears to demonstrate that parents across the range have common priorities when choosing schools. These common factors are:

- child's preference for the school;
- standard of academic education;
- nearness to home/convenience for travel;
- child's happiness at the school.

(Glatter, Woods and Bagley, 1995, p10)

Although Bradley (1996) researched in only one town, he found that the determining factors (as displayed in Table 7.1) tended to relate to the child's happiness, the school's reputation for discipline and academic factors. This backs up the work of Brain and Klein (1994) who found that the key determinants were a happy atmosphere, firm discipline and a good academic reputation.

Table 7.1 Important factors in choice of school

	Factor	%
1	Our child prefers the school.	53
2	We think our child would be happier there.	49
3	The school has a reputation for better discipline.	41
4	The school is in better accommodation and is better equipped.	30
5	It is easier to get to the school.	25
6	The school has a better examination record.	23
7	Our child's friends will attend the school.	22
8	The school makes its pupils work harder.	22
9	The school offers a wide range of courses.	21
10	We prefer the attitude of the school towards uniform.	19

Source: Bradley, 1996, p64; reproduced by permission of the publisher, Carfax Publishing Co, PO Box 25, Abingdon, Oxfordshire OX14 3UE

The evidence from these studies suggest that the clients choose schools based on their individual wants but that these wants do not vary across client groups as much as some people might assume. This reinforces the need to understand the nuances of the potential clients in a particular area (*see* Exercise 7.6).

The needs of the clients

This stage of the strategic market analysis process focuses on the investigation of the *needs* of the various client groups, rather than any *wants* which they might express. It is not always easy to sort out which are the genuine needs because various client groups express their wants loudly.

As the pupils are the primary consumers of the school's product and service, their needs should be the foremost concern. Market research should gather information in order to:

- identify the present needs of pupils in the school, including their needs as defined by the national curriculum legislation and the examination boards;
- identify the future needs of the current pupils;
- identify the needs of those who may enrol, especially if there are anticipated changes in the range of clients.

The main focus of the investigations here is on the educational needs of pupils as defined by the professionals. A wide variety of factors should be examined – for example, teaching and learning approaches, curriculum content and interpersonal factors such as socialisation. While pupil ability is a significant factor in influencing needs, caution is required: pupil potential should be considered, rather than current achievement being seen as a limiting factor. Exercise 7.7 provides some prompts to explore the professionals' view of pupil needs.

The wider national and international society can more easily be seen as clients of the education system as a whole rather than of a particular school. Society determines a set of needs in relation to the school's output and its impact on that society and this must be borne in mind by the schools when developing and communicating their product and service.

The behaviour and activities of the clients

It is important to understand something of the way in which the clients in each segment relate to the community and the value which they attach to education. This will result in the building up of a profile of clients and potential clients. Schools need to know the answers to the following questions in particular:

- How and where do clients and potential clients hear about the school?
- When do they choose the school or develop links with it?
- What opportunities are there to develop relationships with clients and potential clients?

We would not recommend that every school should gather large amounts of data on every client group. A more realistic approach would be to focus on particular groups according to the school's priority needs. For example, a school which has difficulty recruiting staff may wish to investigate whether people are likely to move to the area to take up a post or to be local and, in either case, to determine where these potential applicants would be most likely to see an advertisement or hear about a post. A school which is trying to recruit more pupils from a particular geographical area may wish to investigate whether the potential pupils and parents visit local libraries, community centres and so on and whether or not they would be likely to visit an open evening at the school or whether effort should be targeted on reaching them in their homes. This information will help the school to manage communications and to target promotion at key times of the year and in particular locations.

Bradley (1996) investigated how clients heard about the schools at upper-school entry in one town. He tabulated the sources of information which parents used and their ranking of the usefulness of each source (*see* Table 7.2).

Table 7.2 Sources of information and their usefulness

Source	*Those who used the source (%)*	*Those who found source useful (%)*	*Those using the source who ranked it 'most useful' (%)*
Visits, meetings at school	93	78	84
Brothers or sisters at the school	39	27	69
Their own experience of the school	36	23	65
Parents of pupils	57	32	57
School brochures, booklets	82	38	47
Published 'league tables'	28	10	37
Teachers in the school	33	11	35
Friends or neighbours	42	14	32
Other children at the school	26	8	29
Teachers in a child's present school	9	2	20
Newspapers	8	1	11

Source: Bradley, 1996, p63; reproduced by permission of the publisher, Carfax Publishing Co, PO Box 25, Abingdon, Oxfordshire OX14 3UE

Although it would be possible to gather this type of primary data in your area, it is time-consuming. Exercise 7.8 provides some simple ideas to follow up the question of how parents hear about the school.

Conclusion

When analysing the client market, four factors which we have discussed in the book need to be constantly borne in mind. First, schools need to reflect carefully on the information that already exists in the school and to consider the use of primary and secondary information. The research we use in this chapter by Bradley is a good example of the former. However, much information, such as changing recruitment patterns, can be discerned from postcodes contained in pupil records. Second, the difference between overt and covert information is one that needs to be constantly borne in mind. Parents who visit the school and strongly articulate their views may not be representative of the majority of the parents. This is crucial in establishing what it is that parents prioritise and not what we think they prioritise. The third key factor is that we should base managerial decisions on reliable information and not on the assumptions of the decision-makers. Finally, the often intractable gulf between client wants and educational needs has to be carefully managed. We hope that this chapter has provided a useful framework for analysing clients. If this is done while bearing in mind the four points outlined in this conclusion, then we think much valuable marketing information can be gained.

References

Bradley, H. (1996) 'Parental choice of schools in an area containing grant-maintained schools', *School Organisation,* 16(1), pp 59–69.

Brain, J. and Klein, R. (1994) 'Parental choice: myth or reality?', *Bath Social Policy Papers No 21,* Bath, University of Bath.

Glatter, R., Woods, P. and Bagley, C. (1995) *Diversity, differentiation and hierarchy: school choice and parental preferences,* ESRC/CEPAM Invitation Seminar, Milton Keynes, 7–8 June.

Ries, A. and Trout, J. (1994) *The 22 Immutable Laws of Marketing,* London, HarperCollins.

West, A. (1992) 'Factors affecting choice of school for middle-class parents: implications for marketing', *Educational Management and Administration,* 20(4), pp 223–30.

Exercise 7.1 Identifying your market segments

Study the following market segments. With your own school in mind, add new ones (including those which might offer potential in the future) and delete any which are inappropriate.

1 **Internal markets:**
- Governors
- Staff (teaching and support)
- Regular visitors and helpers
- Current pupils
- Current parents

2 **External markets:**
- Prospective pupils
- Prospective parents
- Former pupils
- Prospective staff
- Other educational institutions (especially the next stage of education)
- The local community
- Commerce and industry
- The Local Education Authority /Funding Agency
- OFSTED
- TTA
- National groups and organisations

3 **Future market segments:**

Exercise 7.2 The internal market

The importance of internal clients is stressed throughout this book. This exercise focuses on the significance of these clients as ambassadors of the school. Consider each of the client groups in the table below. Assess the value of each group as ambassadors of the school using the following scale:

- A Very significant
- B Significant
- C Not very significant

Identify in what way each of the client groups might contribute to the marketing of the school.

Internal targets	*Value*	*Contribution*
Governors (You may wish to subdivide by type.)		
Teaching staff (You may wish to subdivide by type.)		
Support staff • Classroom support • Clerical • Technical • Caretaking • Cleaning • Lunchtime supervisors		

Internal targets	*Value*	*Contribution*
Regular visitors and helpers (It is helpful to list the various types.)		
Current pupils Year ____ Year ____ Year ____ Year ____ Year ____ Year ____ Year ____		
Current parents		
Others		

Exercise 7.3 Mapping the recruitment area

Using a large-scale map of your recruitment area and map pins or similar, indicate the area where each child (or each group of ten children) lives.

A further refinement would be to colour code by year group, as this could identify trends such as:

- an area being 'lost' (indicated by only the oldest age groups living there);
- an area becoming a source of pupils (indicated by mostly younger pupils living there);
- the use of transport routes;
- the transfer of pupils at certain key points to other provision – for example after nursery, going to a primary school nearer to home; sixth formers going elsewhere or transferring in.

A similar but less detailed exercise can be carried out for the competitors.

Exercise 7.4 The recruitment area

This exercise leads on from Exercise 7.3. The questions asked here are significant in any country such as the UK where parents exercise their rights under open enrolment legislation. If the information is to be used effectively, it is important to gather specific data, especially in response to questions 3 and 4.

1 Where is the school's traditional recruitment area?
2 How many pupils have you recruited recently from outside this traditional area?
3 How many pupils out of this traditional area attend other schools?
4 What are the reasons for these shifts in recruitment patterns?

Exercise 7.5 The national wants or expectations

1 What experiences does society (globally, nationally or locally) perceive that schools should provide for the community?
2 What are the main qualities that the next phase of education perceives that pupils should display?
3 What are the main qualities that society perceives that pupils should display in order to be employable?

Exercise 7.6 Parent and pupil wants or expectations

The following can be used to assess parent and pupil wants of the school. The format could easily be adapted to cover other client groups.

1 What do parents perceive that they want from the school?
2 How does this vary across different parts of the locality, ability ranges and so on?
3 What are the pupils' wants and expectations from the school?
4 How does this vary across different parts of the locality, ability ranges and so on?
5 How do the sets of information differ?

Exercise 7.7 The professionals' views of pupil needs

This exercise considers the general attributes which a pupil should possess when leaving the school. Ask the teaching staff the following questions:

1 What skills should the child have acquired by the time he or she leaves the school?
2 What qualities should the school be developing in each child?
3 What standards of behaviour are desirable?

Exercise 7.8 Hearing about the school

This exercise allows the school to examine client behaviour by investigating the ways in which they hear about the school. It also looks at the school's mechanisms for monitoring this information.

1 Compile a list of the most common ways in which parents hear about the school and its reputation.

(If there is no record of this you could use a postal questionnaire, sending it to all parents of the pupils in the first two year groups.)

2 How do you monitor how the parents find out about the school in the first place?

Does the school secretary ask when they telephone?

Are they asked when they visit the school?

Is the question on any documents which are sent to the parents of new children?

8

■ ■ ■

Analysing the School

Would you want this for your child?

Introduction

A school needs to analyse *what* it is offering currently, before it can reinforce that provision through its marketing strategy or adapt it (through the development planning process) to the marketing challenges which it faces.

As explained in Chapter Four, it is important to find out what the clients think, rather than to make assumptions about what they think. It is also important to recognise that any perceptions which clients have may not reflect the reality in the school. There should be a cautious response to the information gathered so that, where necessary, the school can go on to investigate the reasons for the perceptions and whether there is a need to alter the product or service or just to communicate more effectively with the clients and redefine the perceptions held. Furthermore, different clients and client groups will have a different perception of the same aspect of provision so it is important to gather views from a range of clients otherwise an inappropriate inference could be made. There is no need to cover every aspect of provision and every client otherwise the school will have no time for its core business of teaching and learning! Sometimes a major review will be required across a range of clients, but often a more selective range of issues can be tested using an appropriate sample of clients. This can then be added to the evaluation of the school and its activities from other sources such as curriculum evaluation and external inspection in order to provide an integrated assessment. Often some of the information will be available as secondary data from other work. For example, a local research project on factors affecting choice of schools (such as that by Bradley (1996) covered in Chapter Seven) can highlight particular perceptions about individual schools.

The product and service of a school need to be analysed in their broadest sense. While much of the professional focus will be on the curriculum and assessment, those outside the school may make their judgements based on the effectiveness of communications, pupil behaviour and the possession by the pupils of basic and social skills. In planning an analysis of its product and service, all the school's provision should be listed, especially bearing in mind those areas which the clients feel are its significant activities. This would include:

- the formal curriculum;
- assessment and testing;
- results;
- extra-curricular activities;
- pupil discipline and appearance;
- relationships;
- resources;
- staff skills and abilities.

Various approaches and techniques can be employed to gather and analyse perceptions of what the school is offering. This chapter will concentrate on the following:

- a SWOT analysis (strengths, weaknesses, opportunities and threats);
- professional evaluation instruments;
- league tables and other performance indicators;
- questionnaires;
- focus groups and interviews;
- various other sources.

The chief purpose of all these approaches is to develop awareness within the school of clients' perceptions and to manage an appropriate response to the findings, thus building a positive relationship with the clients. Most of the approaches could be used with any of the school's clients except for the professional evaluation instruments which are designed for use by professional educators within the school.

The information gathered in this analysis will enable the school to carry out the following:

To examine its image – that is, the clients' views of the general strengths and weaknesses of the school. The clients in the various market segments (including the staff) will have different views which may have to be reconciled if one corporate image of the school is to be projected.

To monitor client satisfaction with specific aspects of the present provision. How satisfied are current pupils and parents about specific aspects of the curriculum? How effective are home-school links and communications? What is the effectiveness of the newsletter?

To monitor the public perception of the quality of the educational product and the service. How do the next phase of education and the employers perceive children who come from the school?

To assess changes in the attitudes to the school of the clients in each segment.

To identify a wide range of views concerning the potential opportunities and threats that may be presented in the future.

To examine the potential for growth. What is the potential to expand the provision which the school is offering? Is this provision purely to be seen as educational or is the school able to broaden its services – for example, by starting parenthood classes or foreign language courses for commerce and industry?

To identify any evidence of potential decline. What is happening and why and, most significantly, can any decline be reversed by changing the school's emphasis?

To monitor market awareness and attitude. How much awareness, knowledge and interest is there in each market segment concerning the school and its activities? This will help the school to monitor its current marketing approaches.

To identify resource/income generation potential. What opportunities are there to expand the school's financial and other resources?

SWOT analysis

In the commercial/industrial world significant use is made of a SWOT (**s**trengths, **w**eaknesses, **o**pportunities and **t**hreats) analysis which focuses on key aspects of an organisation. This approach is increasingly being used in the public sector and, in particular, in the educational world. It can be used as a method of drawing together information from a variety of techniques – a macro approach, as we describe in Chapter Nine. In this chapter we are going to use it at the micro level for initial information gathering and, as such, it is normally aimed at the level of the whole school. However, it can easily be applied at a sub-group level – for example a department or year group.

A SWOT analysis is straightforward to carry out because it simply involves compiling four lists. It can be undertaken by a variety of people – staff, senior management, governors, pupils, parents and so on. If the SWOT analysis originates from the teaching staff, it is better if the other partners are *asked* for their perceptions rather than simply having assumptions made about the way in which they might view the school. Figure 8.1 shows a typical SWOT form layout that can be used in a school. The form can be completed in several ways to obtain the necessary information. Staff can be asked to fill it in on an individual basis, recording their personal opinions of the school's strengths,

	STAFF PERCEPTIONS	CLIENT PERCEPTIONS
STRENGTHS		
WEAKNESSES		
OPPORTUNITIES		
THREATS		

Fig 8.1 Specimen layout for a SWOT analysis

weaknesses, opportunities and threats. This information can then be collated by senior management. Even better staff can be asked to share their views once the initial form has been completed. They can articulate in groups individual perceptions and then come to a group consensus. In this way a very strong commitment to articulate strengths and identify areas for action (weaknesses) is formed. The staff then have ownership both of the product and the process and have a responsibility to promote strengths and work on weaknesses. When it comes to assessing other clients' perspectives, the staff can be asked to give their view of how these are similar to or different from their own, but actual sampling of client opinion should also take place with parents, pupils and the wider community being asked to give their views on the four areas. This information can then be fed to senior management and added to information from other sources to give a whole school perspective (*see* Chapter Nine). We can now consider in detail each of the elements in the SWOT analysis. After this, an exemplar is provided of a completed SWOT analysis for a typical school.

Strengths

As the name suggests, these are the things which the school or area does well. Teachers often find it difficult (owing to inbuilt modesty) to articulate their own individual strengths but, in our experience, they are more ready to state school, subject or year-group strengths (*see* Exercise 8.2). The school may take it for granted that it has a good academic record and cares for its pupils. Do the teachers articulate that perspective and do parents and other clients recognise it? For example, if the test or examination pass rate is above the national average, do all the staff know? Do they know by how much? Has this been communicated to the pupils and to other clients?

Having identified certain strengths, the school must, at a later stage in the marketing cycle, capitalise on them by:

- seeking ways to communicate these strengths to the internal market and the external clients;
- looking for opportunities to apply the successful strategies in other areas;
- ensuring that reinforcement and praise are given;
- ensuring that such activities receive continued support. (Should these perceived strengths now appear to the senior management team to be activities which need phasing out, the change will need very careful handling!)

Our experience from running many training days in schools is that it is not always easy to articulate precisely what the strengths are. Exercise 8.1 provides an example of comparing the views of staff with the views of different client groups in the internal market. Very often we have found that the two perspectives are not all that fundamentally different, but that there is a differing emphasis and articulation. It is important that these views are integrated in such a way as to provide a consistent message about the school.

Weaknesses

Again, as the name suggests, these are self-explanatory – the things which the school or part of the school does badly. A possible problem here is that staff may be unwilling to articulate problems if they believe that there is an element of accountability present. Realistic self-evaluation or team evaluation will be minimal in such circumstances. Staff will not be honest about themselves and all weaknesses will be of other areas and activities. They need to feel that there is a sense of trust and that what they say will not be used out of context. It is therefore important to have the right context and climate before starting a SWOT analysis. Often schools may prefer to use the term 'areas for development' so as to avoid the negative or critical application of 'weaknesses'.

Having identified certain weaknesses, it will be necessary to formulate a plan to overcome them. This is where the marketing process overlaps with the quality control of the educational product. However, it may be that those who identified the weaknesses were only *perceiving* a problem which did not, in fact, exist. For example, parents may feel that there are not enough textbooks in a particular subject area when, in fact, much of the source material is to be found in attractive, up-to-date booklets which are produced by the school or is obtained from computer-based learning resources. In such cases, communication with the parents needs to be improved.

Opportunities

These are potential openings which could be grasped in the future. If the school or area does not identify these as early as possible, it will not be able to plan resources so that the opportunities can be grasped at the appropriate time. Another school could be more far-sighted and gain an advantage.

To list the opportunities, it is necessary to have a clear view of the environment in which the school will operate in the medium to long term. Nothing is static; the educational world has changed very radically over the last ten years and will continue to do so. There is a need to be creative and so a broad perspective is required. Outsiders to the school or section of it will be helpful in determining the likely opportunities that may be presented in the future. Once the opportunities have been listed, the school can prioritise them for immediate action in the short term or for longer-term consideration. In order to prioritise, the school will have to consider which opportunities will be lost if they are not grasped relatively quickly and which ones the school can afford to develop more slowly.

Threats

As with the identification of possible opportunities, there needs to be some degree of vision about the future educational environment if potential threats to the school or section of it are to be highlighted in plenty of time so that they can be countered. Having identified certain potential threats and people's perceptions of the threats, it is important to take action to avoid them and, better still, to turn such threats into opportunities. For example, a school threatened with the loss of some of its playing fields for building land could simply campaign against this. More positively, it could build links with community organisations so that the land was seen locally as a community asset and less 'dispensable'. As well as acting to minimise the threats, the school needs to adapt its marketing strategy to turn any negative feelings into positive ones within the clients' minds.

The advantages of the SWOT approach are:

- It can be applied at the whole school or area level.
- It is quick and easy to carry out.
- No form of special skill or equipment is required to carry it out or to analyse it.

The possible drawbacks of the SWOT analysis are:

- It gathers very subjective views.
- It encourages fault-finding.
- The results can be diverse and therefore cannot easily be summarised or aggregated.
- It is not weighted so that minor and major issues may be given equal prominence.

An example of a SWOT analysis for a school

Figure 8.2 shows a SWOT analysis of a school. The teaching staff completed one column of the form and the parent governors and representatives of the PTA completed the other. This activity took place when the parental representatives joined the teachers on a training day which dealt with marketing the school. We will now comment on some of the categories and compare the responses by the two groups.

Strengths

It is interesting how the different groups prioritise different items. School staff often assume that the academic quality is good but do not emphasise how well the pupils perform in tests and examinations. However, this is often a significant factor for parents (as shown by research studies such as Glatter *et al*, 1995 and Bradley, 1996), not only at the point of choosing a school but also to

	STAFF PERCEPTIONS	CLIENT PERCEPTIONS
STRENGTHS	Well qualified, committed staff Caring environment Wide range of extra-curricular activities Stable staff	Good exam/test results Music provision Attractive brochure Sports facilities Stable staff
WEAKNESSES	Inconsistent disciplinary procedures State of fabric of building Small classrooms Application of equal opportunities policy Lack of career development Provision for gifted pupils Links with governors	Uniform rules not strict enough Making phone contact in a morning Erratic homework Pupils not stretched enough Classes too large
OPPORTUNITIES	Adult learners Crèche on site Letting the premises	Wider community links Sponsorship
THREATS	Difficulty recruiting certain staff High cost of current staff Senior management time used on administration Neighbouring school's marketing campaign	Poor quality entrants to the teaching profession Resource shortages Effect of national politics

Fig 8.2 A completed SWOT analysis for a school

reinforce their decision as the pupil moves through the school. The availability of league tables has reinforced this performance indicator in the minds of the parents. Schools must recognise this parental want, giving it due priority and publicity in order to maximise the perceived strength. The discussion earlier in the book about overt and covert performance indicators is one to bear in mind in this respect. Good test and examination results are obviously perceived as an overt performance indicator of the school's strength by parents whereas in the next section covert factors, such as school uniform, play a part in the perceived weaknesses of the school.

Weaknesses

Clients' perceptions of the school's weaknesses can be split into things that can be adjusted easily – for example, organising better telephone access – and those which need more concerted activity – for example, extending the pupils academically. It is also important to note the way in which school uniform figures significantly in parental opinion. Similarly, with weaknesses perceived by the staff, some can obviously be attended to more easily – such as strengthening links with the governors – while some aspects – such as a more coherent career development framework – will involve significant management action over a longer timeframe. Having identified the weaknesses, the school will not only have to work to reduce them, but also to communicate its actions to the clients so that their perceptions are changed.

Opportunities

Seeking the opinion of wider client groups has provided a range of ideas. Amalgamation of the two lists will provide a valuable agenda for investigation and action in order to exploit the school's potential and to communicate this more widely.

Threats

Some of these are national issues and are therefore difficult for an individual school to deal with – for example, graduates' poor perception of teaching as a career. However, there are things that the school can do to limit the damage, such as ensuring that its own image and its recruitment process are carefully managed. The underfunding of education has led to resource shortages but there is little which a school can do in the short term to improve overall national funding. However, specific grants or private finance initiatives may produce significant gains for the individual school, especially at secondary level. Recognition of resource shortages may lead to a consideration of sponsorship as an alternative source of revenue. The final threat on the list – the marketing campaign of the neighbouring school – can be countered with the help of the techniques described in this book.

This analysis is based on the value judgements of the participants and needs careful consideration by senior management as it is collated with the other information gathered in the strategic market analysis process.

Professional evaluation instruments

As the title suggests, professional evaluation instruments are the approaches which are used by professionals in the school in order to assess what the school currently has to offer in terms of its product and service. It is possible to choose from a variety of techniques such as Guidelines for Review and Internal Development in Schools (GRIDS) (Abbott *et al*, 1988) and Diagnosis of Individual and Organisational Need (DION) (Elliott-Kemp and Williams, 1980) for evaluating the school's activities. Some of these (such as DION) can be carried out and analysed quite quickly but others involve a gradual process of determining problems and identifying priority areas for improvement.

Evaluations carried out by other professionals such as OFSTED and LEA inspectors can also provide significant instruments for evaluation and improvement. Any of these instruments can form part of the normal process of evaluating a school's activities but they are also valuable in that they provide information to feed into the marketing process. Part of the OFSTED process involves the gathering of information from parents and the results of the inspection must be disseminated to the parents of current pupils and be made available to the general public, including the media. Careful handling of the findings can ensure that the school promotes its successful points and limits the damage of any weaknesses found.

League tables and other performance indicators

Many performance indicators are available internally, through the media or through the OFSTED data analysis process (available through the Internet). These cover aspects such as unit costs, the results of pupils' tests and examinations, attendance and absence. These can be analysed by the school not only to determine areas for action but also to decide which strengths to promote through the marketing process.

Questionnaires

The school may wish to use this approach for a major review, for a regular annual review or just to gather information about a limited aspect of provision. Once the school has identified the area of activity about which it wishes to sample the clients and/or professionals, a questionnaire can be designed which will elicit the required information. This can be carried out by post, by telephone or through personal interviews. The main benefits of this approach are:

- attention can be focused on the particular area of information which the school requires;
- it collects primary information direct from the clients;
- it covers a broad sample of clients so that generalisations and inferences can be drawn.

The drawbacks of using this approach mainly centre on:

- the time needed to draw up and administer the questionnaire and to analyse the data;
- the expense of the materials and of the time needed;
- the delay in obtaining the information.

These drawbacks emphasise the need for careful planning of the investigation (as outlined in Chapter Four) so that information needs are focused and so that, where appropriate, information for a variety of purposes can be obtained at the same time. For example, if the school particularly needs information on its arrangements for parents' evenings or on the reasons why parents have not chosen the school, then a short questionnaire can be devised to a defined sample and it will be easier to collect the returns and to collate the data. An example of such as approach is given in Exercise 8.3. If, on the other hand, the school wishes to have a major review, then a much larger exercise is required. It is still possible, with careful planning, to minimise the workload – for example, by using an optical mark reader to analyse the data.

Several major research projects could usefully be adapted by schools. We would draw attention to the following in particular:

- Work with (mainly) Scottish schools by Macbeath *et al* (1996) published by the NUT which focuses on parents and school effectiveness.
- Work by Joan Ruddock *et al* (1995) which focuses on listening to the pupils' perspectives on schools.
- The Open University's PASCI study (Glatter *et al*, 1995) mentioned in Chapter Seven.

An example of the questionnaire approach

We use here the example of a longitudinal study which we have been carrying out as a research project over the last five years (*see* Davies and Ellison, 1995) in order to analyse the perceptions of schools' pupils, parents and staff. Thirty questions are randomised in the questionnaire but are regrouped for analysis as follows:

For pupils and parents

Quality of teaching and learning

Satisfaction with staff

Communications

Standards of student behaviour

Quality of school facilities

General factors and overall satisfaction

Equal opportunities for students

(or, for parents, the role of the governors in the school)

For teachers

Communications in the school

Quality of the working environment for the staff

Professional environment in the school

Quality of education supplied by the school

Professional support offered to teachers

Role of the governing body

General satisfaction with the school

The results are tabulated for each client group and are presented by category, a sample of which is shown in Table 8.1. Additional comments made by the clients are summarised so as to preserve anonymity.

Table 8.1 Sample parent response in the teaching and learning category (%)

		Yes	*No*	*Not sure*
1	Do you feel that the school is offering the right type of education for your child?	88	3	9
4	Do you feel that your child is sufficiently challenged by the school to encourage maximum learning and development?	53	28	19
11	Do you feel that the number of students in your child's classes is appropriate?	67	22	11
18	Do you feel that your child is set the right type of homework?	58.5	34.5	7
15	Do you feel that your child is set the right amount of homework?	62	32	6
	Average for this section	65.7	23.9	10.4

All the schools in the project began by analysing the perceptions of the teaching staff but some have now used an adjusted questionnaire (*see* the end of Appendix 2) to cover all the staff including lunchtime assistants. This integration of the staff reflects our comments in earlier chapters about the significance and value of all staff and the building of a marketing culture. If a questionnaire covers all staff, then it is important to ensure that all have a good understanding of the areas covered by the questions, otherwise some feel disenfranchised through lack of knowledge. Such a questionnaire cannot cover some of the in-depth issues as easily as a more focused one to the teaching staff but supplementary questions could be added or follow-up discussions could allow for more specific comments.

The full set of questions in each category is given in Appendix 1 and the randomised questionnaires are given in Appendix 2.

Although most of our research schools in this part of the project were secondary schools, the process has also been undertaken at primary level. The questions for the parents and staff do not present a problem here but a lot of work has been done to make the pupil questionnaire accessible down to Year 1. This involves the pupils receiving some assistance from teaching and support staff who will need some training so as to ensure that the process is as valid as possible. Questions also require some modification. The implementation of this approach with Years 1 and 2 is described by a primary headteacher in Appendix 3.

The surveys allow schools to gather information from a representative group rather than relying on that gained from vociferous parents or pupils either at the supportive or critical ends of the spectrum. As discussed in earlier chapters, current pupils and their parents are very significant influencers of 'decisions to buy', so it is important to have an accurate up-to-date view of their perceptions. The staff questionnaire provides a more honest view of the staff's perceptions than almost any other method. There are always problems with anonymity when canvassing staff opinion so we have often received and analysed the staff questionnaire ourselves to assure confidentiality.

Results in different categories need to be interpreted very carefully and appropriate responses provided. In Table 8.1 the Yes response of 67 per cent shows some dissatisfaction with class size. It may be that the school employs significant additional help in the classroom and that this needs to be communicated more effectively through the marketing strategy.

Focus groups and interviews

Focus groups are a very useful way of gathering information about a specific issue or from a specific set of clients. They can also be used to follow up issues raised in a questionnaire or to provide a general way of giving clients a chance to comment on the school and its work.

Care is needed to ensure that those attending are representative in relation to the investigation. For example, if the groups are held while parents are attending a parents' evening, then care must be taken with validity as there are certain individuals or groups who may not attend such events or who may not be able to spare the extra time required.

One of our research schools has used this approach very successfully. The head has chaired informal discussions at various school events and, as well as gathering information about perceptions, he has been able to demonstrate to the parents that they are valued clients.

There are a variety of ways of carrying out *interviews*. As we have discussed elsewhere, short telephone calls to clients such as parents and school neighbours, perhaps comprising three questions, can allow them to raise issues which are relatively minor so that the school can deal with them before they become major problems. More detailed interviews with clients can be used to follow up information gleaned in general questionnaires. One of our research schools offered parents the opportunity to put their names on a major questionnaire so that there could be some follow up. This resulted in the senior management team making phone calls to follow up issues raised by about 50 of a secondary school's families.

Various other sources

Many sources of secondary data are available to build up a picture of client perceptions. One example is the evidence which pupils write as they transfer into a school. Those responsible for the induction of new pupils often use questionnaires and quizzes which ask how the pupil feels about the new school. Most English departments in secondary schools ask new pupils to write about their first days in the school. If a school allows its pupils to prepare an alternative prospectus, this can be a useful source of information about the perceptions of the existing pupils. Perhaps the most important information here is the perceptions which the pupils are banned from including in the alternative prospectus!

Conclusion

A wider range of perceptions of the school can be combined with internal evaluation approaches used by professionals to provide a clear picture of what the school is offering or, more significantly, is perceived as offering. Only then can this evidence be analysed in the context of what the market wants and a reconciliation be attempted.

References

Abbott, R., Steadman S. and Birchenhough M. (1988) *GRIDS School Handbooks*, 2nd edn, primary and secondary versions, York, Longman for the SCDC.

Bradley, H. (1996) 'Parental choice of schools in an area containing grant-maintained schools', *School Organisation*, 16(1), pp 59–69.

Davies, B. and Ellison, L. (1995) 'Improving the quality of the school – ask the clients?', *School Organisation*, 15(1).

Elliott-Kemp, J. and Williams, G.L. (1980) *The DION handbook: diagnosis of individual and organisational need*, Sheffield, Sheffield Polytechnic Education Department.

Glatter, R., Woods, P. and Bagley, C. (1995) *Diversity, differentiation and hierarchy: school choice and parental preferences*, ESRC/CEPAM Invitation Seminar, Milton Keynes, 7–8 June.

Macbeath, J. *et al* (1996) *Schools speak for themselves*, London, National Union of Teachers.

Ruddock, J., Chaplain, R. and Wallace, G. (1995) *School improvement: what can pupils tell us?*, London, David Fulton.

Exercise 8.1 Staff analysis of strengths and weaknesses

Most schools have considerable autonomy to manage their own affairs. One key element in the success of this is how well the school relates to its local community and communicates the positive things that it does. In this context fill in the questionnaire below:

1 Give three or four strengths and weaknesses of your school.
2 Write down three or four strengths and weaknesses of your school as perceived by parents.
3 Are the strengths and weaknesses perceived differently by the pupils in your school? Give examples.
4 Would you send your child to your school? If so, why? If not, why not?
5 Would you recommend a colleague to work at your school?

Exercise 8.2 Strengths and weaknesses of an area of the school

Teachers should fill in the questionnaire below:

1 Give three or four strengths and weaknesses of your key stage, year group or department.
2 Write down three or four strengths and weaknesses of your key stage, year group or department as perceived by other colleagues in your school.
3 Write down three or four strengths and weaknesses of your key stage, year group or department as perceived by parents (using information gained through market research).
4 Are the strengths and weaknesses perceived differently by the pupils in your school? Give examples.

Exercise 8.3 Parental involvement in the primary school

This questionnaire was designed by Max Amesbury to be quick and simple for busy parents, yet it should provide the information which the school requires.

COMMUNICATION	
1 Does the school newsletter sent out each month give you:	
enough information?	YES/NO
the right kind of information?	YES/NO
2 If 'no' to either question, please give any suggestions about how it could be improved.	
3 Do the letters about trips give you:	
enough information?	YES/NO
the right kind of information?	YES/NO
4 If 'no' to either question, please give any suggestions about how it could be improved	

VISITING SCHOOL

5 Do you consider that the school makes you feel welcome when you come into school?

6 If 'yes' is there anything in particular that makes you feel welcome?

7 If no, how could we improve the situation?

HELPING

8 If given the opportunity would you like to help in school?

YES/NO

9 If yes, please tick the tasks mentioned that you would enjoy doing.

Reading with my child	☐	Assisting with computers	☐
Reading with other children	☐	Helping on trips	☐
Helping with art	☐	Reading a story	☐

If you have any other comments about parental involvement, please write them in the space below.

Thank you

9

Integrating and Interpreting the Marketing Evidence

'So what does it all mean?'

Introduction

It is now important to bring together all the marketing information which was gained through using the framework outlined in Chapters Five to Eight in order to inform the creation of the marketing strategy for implementation. This involves an aggregation of the information gained relating to the school's business, its competitors and the world in which it operates in order to highlight the key strategic factors from a macro point of view. This we do using a case study format which shows five techniques: SWOT analysis; Boston Consulting Group matrix; General Electric Screen; Little's lifecycle portfolio analysis; and Kawasaki's matrix. Our experience has shown these five techniques, used singly or in combination, to be very valuable. Once the information has been brought together using these techniques, it will be possible for governors and senior managers to identify areas for action. Those responsible for planning and implementing the marketing strategy can then be briefed on the key requirements (*see* Chapter Eleven).

Each of the techniques is now described in detail and an example is given of using each one in practice.

SWOT analysis

In Chapter Eight we described the use of a SWOT format in gathering the perceptions of the various client groups. Here we make use of the same tool in a different way – to compile a macro picture from all the evidence in Chapters

Five to Eight. This does not simply involve filling in the details from the data, but requires that senior leaders in the school consider the validity of the data gathered thus ensuring the value of the information provided. It is a more rational approach than the subjective use of the tool in Chapter Eight.

The SWOT form in Fig 9.1 was compiled by one of the schools in our research project. It brings together information from a variety of sources and provides an overall summary.

Figure 9.2 is a blank SWOT form which could be used to bring together the information from a strategic market analysis.

	STRENGTHS	WEAKNESSES
STAFF	Committed, stable, dedicated, enthusiastic, professional, supportive, hard-working, teamworking, empowered faculty and department heads	Some poor teachers and some poor departments; too many inexperienced staff; some staff failing to take responsibilities
MANAGEMENT	Head experienced, SMT experienced and enthusiastic	Issues across all staff; policy inconsistencies in application; communication; work pressure; cohesiveness; lack of vision and mission sense
PUPILS	Recent achievements; split-site – good for pupils	Gender imbalance; low ability
FINANCES		Poor decoration and repair of buildings
ETHOS	Growing school reputation	Problems within ethos, e.g. discipline; attendance; litter
GOVERNORS	Maturing body	Poor image

Fig 9.1 Macro SWOT analysis for Rivergate School

	OPPORTUNITIES	THREATS
PUPILS	Higher ability intake; full recruitment; able to exploit other schools' weaknesses reduce to 7 form entry	Overcapacity in the system; gender imbalance continues
OFSTED	Opportunity for improvement	Bad press, league tables
INTERNAL	Improving exam results and standards; improved environment; opportunity to be a model school	
EXTERNAL		Pupil dumping from other schools; pupil career opportunities (lack of); aggressive parents
FUTURE		Staff turnover; ageing staff; unresolved issues, e.g. punctuality and attendance
MORALE	Feel-good factor; new ethos new partnerships; good publicity; sports centre	Lack of clear criteria in planning; competing agendas; self-congratulatory; fall in enthusiasm

Fig 9.1 continued

	STRENGTHS	WEAKNESSES
CURRICULUM		
EXTRA-CURRICULAR ACTIVITIES		
RESOURCES		
STAFF		
GOVERNORS		
RESULTS		
ETHOS		
OTHER		

Fig 9.2 Blank SWOT matrix

	OPPORTUNITIES	THREATS
OTHER PROVIDERS		
LEGISLATION		
TECHNOLOGY		
DEMOGRAPHIC TRENDS		
EMPLOYMENT TRENDS		
ECONOMIC TRENDS		

Fig 9.2 continued

The BCG matrix

The Boston Consulting Group (BCG) matrix is a method of examining each of an organisation's business units against two criteria. The first criterion relates to the *growth rate of the market* for the product or service being provided and the second criterion relates to the organisation's *current share of that market*. The business unit is then placed in one of the quadrants of a matrix (*see* Fig 9.3) according to whether it is considered to be a star, a cash cow, a problem child or a dog. The process can usefully be adapted to allow schools to draw together information from their analysis (Chapters Five to Eight) and to categorise the key elements.

A *star* is a product or service which has a high market share in a growing market. Examples in schools could be an established nursery or well developed vocational provision at post-16. The school has an advantage over its competitors because it has an established position in the market while others are having to invest heavily in order to enter the market or gain market share. One of the problems associated with a star is that, as the market is still growing, there is a need, even for a market leader, to spend considerable amounts of money on both human and physical resources in order to maintain its market position and to satisfy demand. For this reason, a school's range of activities needs to include some cash cows.

Cash cows are the products or services which have a high market share in a stable market. There is little need to invest in this area as most of the resources are in place. Some of the resources generated are thus available to support the development of the star products and services so that they can become the cash cows of the future. An example of a cash cow in schools could be A level English within Year 12–13 provision or the teaching of seven year olds.

Products and services which fall into the *problem child* category are those which have a low market share in an area where demand is rising. Problem children need to be nurtured along but the process is expensive. There is a high demand for investment in human and physical resources but, at the same time, it is difficult to make as much progress as those schools which already have a high share in the particular market. A good example of this is schools which are trying to provide a range of vocational courses when there are already other schools or colleges in the area with well established provision and expertise. Some schools have found that resource constraints have meant that their cash cows cannot support the vocational 'problem child' and have withdrawn from that particular market. In other cases, a careful nurturing process can result in the problem child becoming a cash cow.

Dogs are those aspects of the school's provision which have a low share in a market which is not growing. Examples might be a particular A level or GCSE subject, or a nursery class in an area of low population growth. The standard approach when a dog product or service has been identified is to withdraw

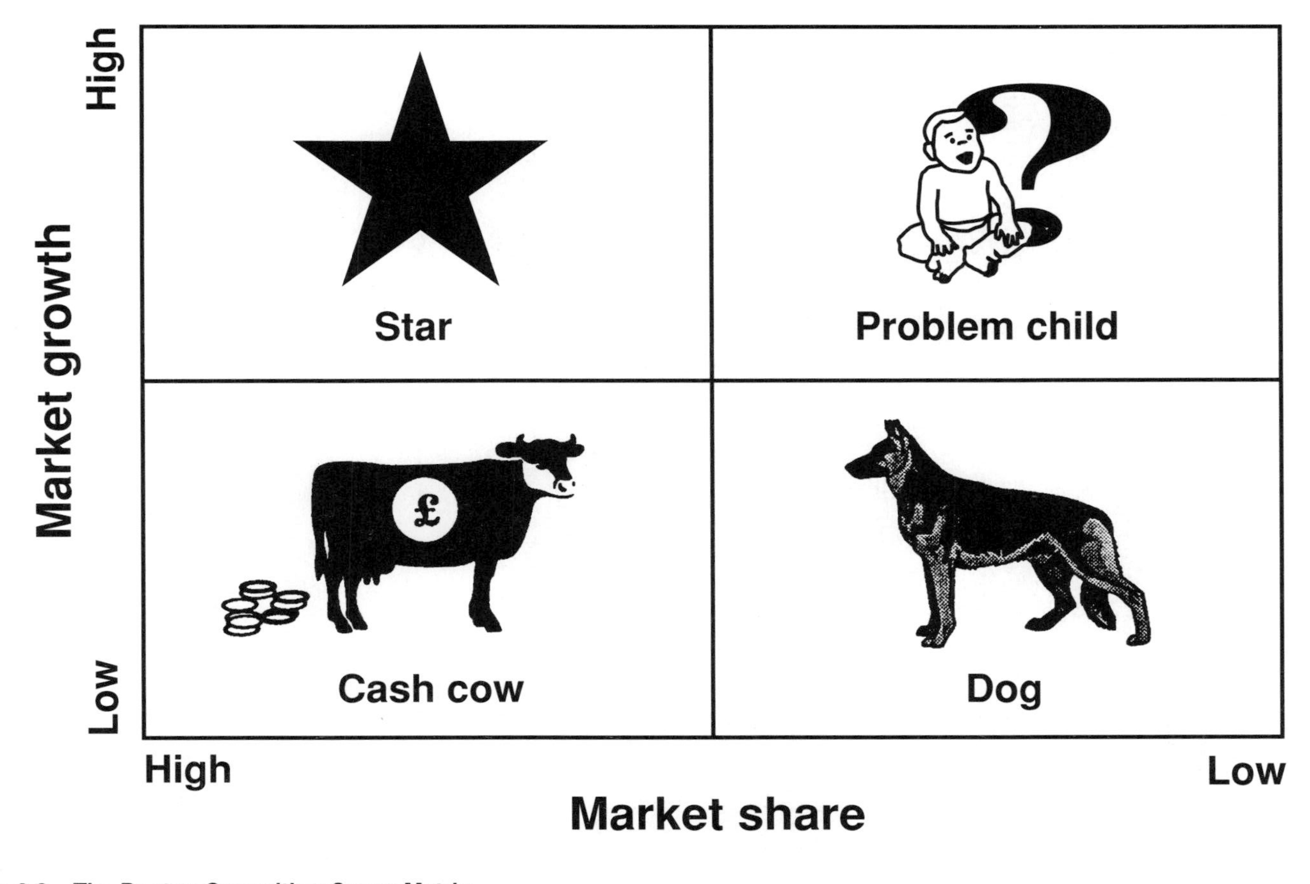

Fig 9.3 The Boston Consulting Group Matrix

from the market. This allows the organisation's resources to be more effectively targeted towards other areas. The decision to withdraw should not be taken too hastily, however, as a particular aspect of the school may complete the product range or provide a credible presence in the market. For example, the dropping of A level Music may cause some pupils to leave and therefore will have a knock-on effect on other A level groups such as French. A primary school which decides to stop providing hot lunches may be seen as uncaring by the parents. It may be wise to retain a dog product in order to keep competitors out of the market or with a view to revitalising the product later.

The BCG matrix can thus be used to analyse present products and services and to build up a picture of how the school compares with other providers of education. Figure 9.4 shows a BCG matrix for post-16 provision.

In the example in Fig 9.4, A level Psychology (a star) was introduced four years ago and has consistently recruited groups of between 18 and 24 and achieved high pass rates. Resourcing levels are not excessive and the school is attracting extra pupils to join the sixth form because it offers this option. GNVQs (a problem child) have received a high level of resourcing in terms of staff training and development, syllabus preparation, material purchase and are recruiting reasonably well. Whether GNVQs can become a star or a cash cow will depend on whether recruitment increases significantly over the next two to three years. In this hope, the school continues to invest in them but at the moment a promising start is waiting to be turned into an outstanding success. A level English (a cash cow) is taught reasonably well with good results and always attracts viable group sizes. The school is well resourced in this area and staff have the necessary expertise so little investment is needed. The products identified as dogs are A levels in Music and Design and Technology. Music has had rapid turnover with several heads of department over the last five years so that results have been poor and parents have a lack of confidence regarding continuity and quality. Design and Technology has never recruited viable

Stars	**Problem children**
A level Psychology	GNVQS
Cash cows	**Dogs**
A level English	A level Music A level Design and Technology

Fig 9.4 An example of a BCG matrix from the secondary sector: post-16 provision

Stars	**Problem children**
Nursery provision After-school information technology workshops	Special needs provision Peripatetic music
Cash cows National curriculum teaching at ages 5 to 11	**Dogs** Provision of hot meals

Fig 9.5 A BCG matrix: primary example

groups at A level and has a high resource cost. This is exacerbated by the fact that a school two miles away has Technology College status and is well resourced in this area with pupils obtaining good results and appearing in the press frequently as they win regional and national awards for their designs.

An example of a BCG matrix for the primary sector is shown in Fig 9.5.

In the example in Fig 9.5, over the last three years the provision of a nursery (a star) has recruited large numbers of pupils who have then stayed on into Key Stage 1 giving a secure base to the school roll. The work that the school had been doing in information technology (a star) has a local and regional reputation and parents regard this as a positive reason for choosing the school. The problem children are two areas where the school is expending significant resources but is yet to obtain either a coherent special needs operation or viable music tradition and recruitment. The cash cows can be considered to be the general teaching of Years 1 to 6 through the national curriculum. The school provides a reasonable standard, as validated by the last OFSTED report, and as a result recruits a high proportion of pupils in its immediate catchment area. School dinners (a dog – but not hot!) are perceived as being unappetising and the service unfriendly so that a large proportion of the children bring sandwiches. As a result, the school meals budget runs at a deficit and is a major financial concern.

The General Electric screen

As with the matrices above, the General Electric (GE) screen (or Industry Attractiveness matrix) is a tool that was developed for use in the industrial/ commercial world but which can usefully guide a school in analysing its position in the market. The screen covers a variety of different factors which are grouped on two axes: sector/market attractiveness and relative business strength.

The axis entitled *'sector/market attractiveness'* covers a number of factors whose key descriptors are:

- market size
- profit margins
- competition
- growth rate
- supplier power.

On the *'relative business strength'* axis are:

- relative market share
- management skills
- product/service quality
- reputation
- location.

A school can consider how its products and services are positioned in relation to each of the descriptors. One of our research case study schools (Towngate) has used this conceptual framework to analyse its activities. Its interpretation of its descriptors is shown in Figs 9.6 and 9.7.

MARKET ATTRACTIVENESS	CRITERIA
School market size	The number of 11 to 16 year olds in the area over the next 5 years
Outcomes of the educational process (profit margins)	Results in • core subjects • all subjects • A*–Cs • A*–Gs
Competition	Other Townborough schools (maintained) Other Townborough schools (GM, CTC) Schools in surrounding LEAs Private schools
Growth rate	Measurements of added value
Client power	Parental attitude Community perspective

Fig 9.6 Market attractiveness criteria for Towngate School

RELATIVE BUSINESS STRENGTH	CRITERIA
Relative market share (catchment area)	Pupil recruitment Pupil turnover Percentage of local pupils attending the school
Management skills	Senior management Middle management Management skills of teachers Support staff
Product/service quality	Quality of teaching and learning
Brand image	Reputation in local and regional community School culture and ethos
Location	The school's environment and its geographical position

Fig 9.7 Relative business strength criteria for Towngate School

The school then used this framework to ask different groups within the school to rate on a scale from 1 to 10 the school's position against each of the descriptors. The scores could be grouped into three bands as follows:

Upper (U)	7–10
Mid-range (M)	4–6
Lower (L)	0–3

The results are shown in Tables 9.1 and 9.2.

Table 9.1 GE screen analysis for Towngate School – market attractiveness

	Senior management team	*Middle managers*	*Parent–Teacher Association*	*Governors*
School market size	7 (U)	8 (U)	6 (M)	6 (M)
Results	5 (M)	7 (U)	7 (U)	4 (M)
Competition	6 (M)	6 (M)	8 (U)	5 (M)
Growth rate	8 (U)	8 (U)	7 (U)	5 (M)
Supplier power	8 (U)	6 (M)	6 (M)	6 (M)

Table 9.2 GE screen analysis for Towngate School – relative business strength

	Senior management team	*Middle managers*	*Parent-Teacher Association*	*Governors*
Relative market share	5 (M)	7 (U)	6 (M)	5 (M)
Management skills	7 (U)	6 (M)	4 (M)	4 (M)
Quality	4 (M)	7 (U)	5 (M)	4 (M)
School culture and ethos	5 (M)	6 (M)	5 (M)	4 (M)
Location	3 (L)	3 (L)	6 (M)	3 (L)

The school can focus on marketing the areas where it scores in the upper range and focusing management attention on the middle and lower range for remedial action for the longer-term strategic marketing strategy.

Little's lifecycle portfolio matrix

This instrument was developed for the world of business and commerce by the business consultants Arthur D. Little and places factors on two axes of a matrix. One axis relates to the *competitive position* of the school in relation to others in the market. The descriptors here range from dominant through strong, favourable and tenable to weak. The second axis relates to the stages of *industrial maturity* as determined by descriptors ranging from embryonic through growth and mature to ageing. Figure 9.8 is a summary of their lifecycle portfolio matrix and Fig 9.9 shows it in matrix form.

COMPETITIVE POSITION	STAGES OF INDUSTRY MATURITY
Dominant • has a legalised monopoly **Strong** • can follow own strategies without concern about the competition **Favourable** • one of several leaders **Tenable** • can be maintained by focus **Weak** • too small to survive independently in the long run	**AS JUDGED AGAINST THE FOLLOWING CRITERIA:** • Market growth rate • Growth potential • Breadth of product lines • Number of competitors • Spread of market share between competitors • Customer loyalty • Entry barriers • Technology **THE STAGES ARE THUS CHARACTERISED AS FOLLOWS:** **Embryonic:** • Rapid growth • Changes in technology • Fragmented market share • Pursuit of new customers **Through growth and mature to:** **Ageing:** • Falling demand • Declining number of customers • Narrow product line

Fig 9.8 Features of Little's lifecycle portfolio matrix

COMPETITIVE POSITION	STAGES OF INDUSTRY MATURITY			
	Embryonic	Growth	Mature	Ageing
Dominant	Fast grow Start-up	Fast grow Attain cost leadership Renew Defend position	Defend position Attain cost leadership Renew Fast grow	Defend position Focus Renew Grow with industry
Strong	Start-up Differentiate Fast grow	Fast grow Catch-up Attain cost leadership Differentiate	Attain cost leadership Renew, focus Differentiate Grow with industry	Find niche Hold niche Hang-in Grow with industry Harvest
Favourable	Start-up Differentiate Focus Fast grow	Differentiate, focus Catch-up Grow with industry	Harvest, hang-in Find niche, hold niche Renew, turnaround Differentiate, focus Grow with industry	Retrench Turnaround
Tenable	Start-up Grow with industry Focus	Harvest, catch-up Hold niche, hang-in Find niche Turnaround Focus Grow with industry	Harvest Turnaround Find niche Retrench	Divest Retrench
Weak	Find niche Catch-up Grow with industry	Turnaround Retrench	Withdraw Divest	Withdraw

Fig 9.9 The Lifecycle Portfolio Matrix

This is represented in matrix form as shown in Fig 9.9. The matrix can be used to plot the position of the school as a whole or to plot a range of the school's products and services so as to determine its response within the context of the market and thus to determine the strategy which the school might consider adopting. For example, if the school has no competitors in the provision of a growth market such as after-school care, then the matrix would suggest a 'fast grow' strategy accompanied by an appropriate marketing drive. On the other hand, if the school has many competitors for the provision of a narrow range of A levels – a mature to ageing market – it may consider withdrawing from the market in the medium term but, in the short term, may decide on additional publicity to try to improve viability.

In the following sections we show the way in which this technique was used to plot two schools and then to plot a specific aspect of two schools' provision.

An independent primary school

The school is seen as being very strong in terms of its leadership, quality of teaching and learning and results. The competitors have cramped sites and results are not good.

There are increasing numbers of pre-school children in the surrounding area, especially in owner-occupied housing where parents have high aspirations for their children. The school has ample grounds and there is good access for parents with cars or on foot. The school offers a wide range of extra-curricular activities and provides after-school care. There are no other independent primary schools in the area. Current parents are very happy with the school and will continue to support and promote it. Expansion will require funding, some of which can be obtained from the school's foundation funds. The increased use of educational technology will support a cost-effective expansion but is unlikely to act as a learning substitute (for example, for learning at home) for pupils in this age range.

We would plot this school at point 1 on the lifecycle portfolio matrix in Fig 9.10 which shows that it is in a strong competitive position and in a growth market. The strategies for this school can be ascertained from Fig 9.9.

A declining secondary school

This 11–18 school has 300 pupils (although its capacity is 800) while the others in the town have 600, 890 and 1350.

The pupil numbers in the primary schools do not suggest any increase in number in the town over the next six years and the main emphasis in local house-building is on starter homes. The school has considerable spare capacity. Only a minimum number of options are available at GCSE and A level. There are three competitors in the town. A town five miles away has five secondary schools, an FE college and a highly regarded independent school. Most other schools are operating at 70 to 100 per cent capacity. The houses in the

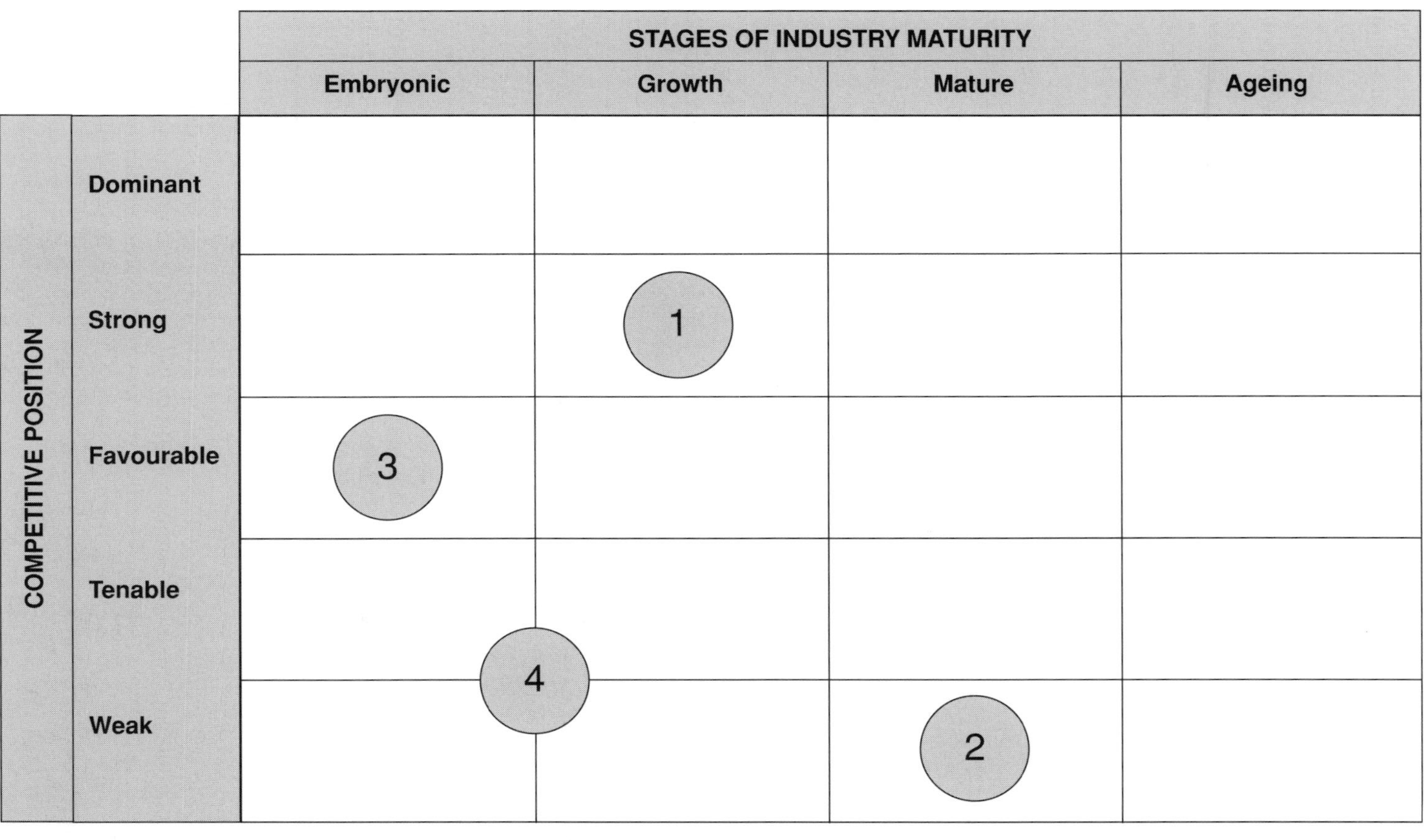

Fig 9.10 Sample positioning on the lifecycle portfolio matrix

immediate area are mature council houses. Their occupants were loyal to the school but their children have now grown up and left the area. The school currently has high fixed costs and finds it difficult to invest and innovate in order to re-enter the market.

On Fig 9.10 we would plot this school at point 2 which shows that it is in a weak competitive position in a mature market. The strategies for this school can be ascertained from Fig 9.9. This puts the school in a very serious position.

Laptop computers in a primary school

The school is one of four which are well respected in the town. The other five schools are perceived to be less effective.

There is a growing demand from parents for extensive use of IT in lessons as many homes have computers. There are many aspects of teaching and learning which can be enhanced by the use of IT and it allows the children to become part of a global classroom through, for example, the Internet. Other schools, including those seen as good ones, are not as far advanced in the area of IT as this one. Parents have confidence in the school and respect the staff's judgement regarding new initiatives. There is a considerable cost if the school is to move to a laptop computer for every child but parental fund-raising and local business sponsorship are likely to be forthcoming.

On Fig 9.10 we would plot this initiative at point 3 which shows that it is in a favourable competitive position in an embryonic market. The appropriate strategies can be ascertained from Fig 9.9.

GNVQ in a secondary school

The school is one of three 13–18 schools in the area and there is an FE college. GNVQ provision is not perceived to be one of the school's strengths.

Although there will be an increase in the number of 16 to 18 year olds over the next five years, there is some doubt about the regard in which GNVQ courses are held. Furthermore, there is an increased demand for school-leavers in local industry and commerce. The school only provides three subjects at GNVQ while the other schools and the college provide a wider range. Parents and pupils are dubious about the quality of the school's provision in this area. There are considerable staff development and equipment requirements if the school is to expand this area.

On Fig 9.10 we would plot this school at point 4 which shows that it is in a weak to tenable competitive position and in an uncertain market which, depending on educational trends, could either expand or fall from favour in the eyes of the clients. The possible strategies for this school can be ascertained from Fig 9.9 but as there are considerable uncertainties it would be important for senior management to be aware of developments in this area.

Kawasaki's matrix

We have found that a useful approach is to use an educational interpretation of Kawasaki's matrix which links a school's ability to provide goods or services with the client's perception of the value of those products or services (*see* Fig 9.11). The matrix has been adapted for an educational setting.

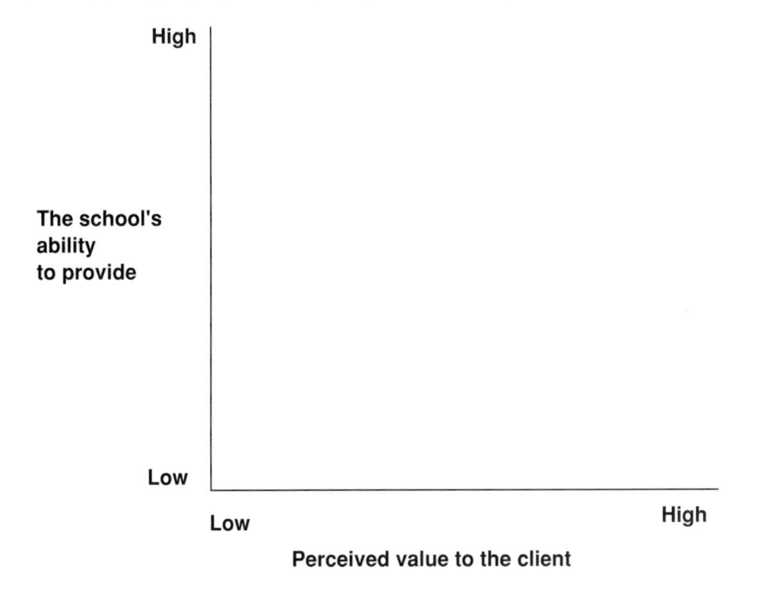

Fig 9.11 Kawasaki's matrix
(*Source*: Davies and Ellison, 1997, p216; adapted from Kawasaki, 1995, p76; itself based on Richey, 1994, pp 47–51. Excerpted by permission of the original publisher, from *The Marketer's Visual Tool Kit* by Terry Richey. © 1994 Timberline Strategies Inc. Published by AMACOM, a division of American Management Association. All rights reserved.)

From the information gathered the school should:

- decide which are the most significant features of the school's 'product' and service;
- position them on the matrix;
- study the position of the features. Those features towards the top right are the ones that can be promoted quite easily as the school is quite successful and the features are valued by clients. Those towards the top left may need a particular focus in the marketing strategy if the client is to change his/her attitude to their value. Those features which appear in the lower part of the matrix must be discussed as part of the school's development planning process.

Consider three examples provided by Deansgate School in their sampling of client opinion.

1 There is a preference for extensive Saturday morning games provision by parents.
2 The parents show a lack of enthusiasm for mixed-ability teaching.
3 The parents want an increased level of computer provision.

The school is in the following position:

- Staff are no longer willing to provide unpaid overtime to supervise Saturday morning games and as a result it is difficult to provide the extensive sports programme that the parents desire (point A on Fig 9.12);
- It can provide mixed ability teaching and has staff trained to do so but there is little parental enthusiasm for it (point B on Fig 9.12);
- It has the ability to spend limited additional resources to enhance the computer provision, but not as much as it feels is necessary to meet all its educational needs and it is aware of parental expectations in this area (point C on Fig 9.12).

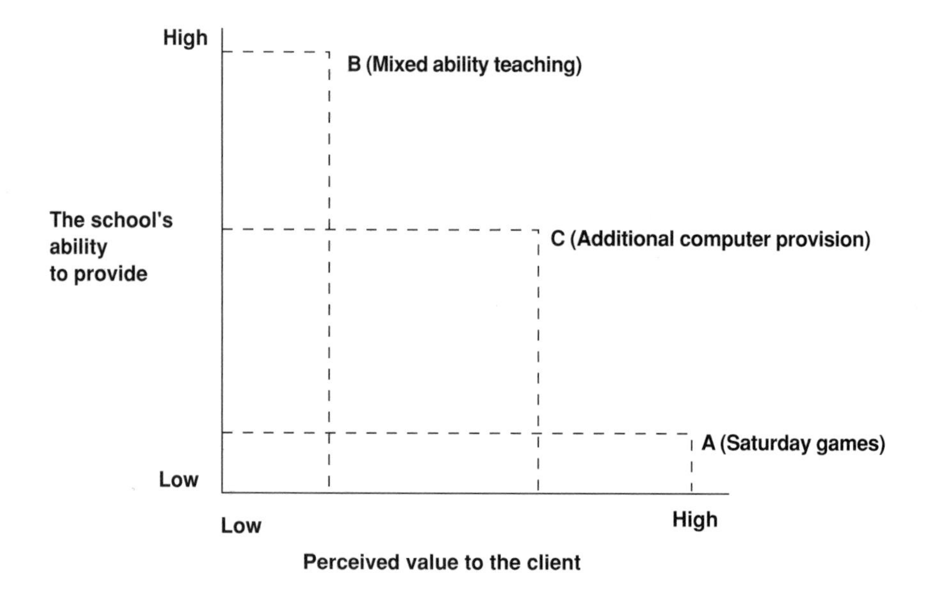

Fig 9.12 Matching provision and parental expectations

Conclusion

This chapter illustrates a variety of ways in which the school can aggregate and interpret the data gathered in Chapters Five to Eight. The next stage involves the judgement of the senior management of the school in assessing the information provided and defining a limited number of key strategic tasks. If the process is to remain focused, we suggest that this be limited to a maximum of four or five. The operationalisation of these strategic tasks can then be delegated to the marketing group for action, as shown in Chapter Eleven.

References

Arthur D. Little. The techniques built around the lifecycle concept have been developed and explained by the consultants Arthur D. Little in a series of booklets, the first of which was Wright, R.V.L. (1974) *A System of Managing Diversity*, Arthur D. Little.

Davies, B. and Ellison, L. (1997) 'Marketing schools: strategic perspectives' in Davies, B. and Ellison, L. (eds) *School Leadership for the 21st Century*, London, Routledge.

Kawasaki, G. (1995) *How to Drive your Competition Crazy*, New York, Hyperion.

Richey, T. (1994) *The Marketer's Visual Tool Kit*, New York: American Management Association.

PART FOUR

Marketing Implementation

10 Marketing Techniques and Approaches *143*

11 Implementing the Marketing Plan *181*

12 Evaluating the Marketing Process *193*

10

Marketing Techniques and Approaches

Take out your socket set and ratchet up for action

Introduction

Before any decision is taken on the marketing strategy to be used to promote the school's product and service, there has to be a review of the range of appropriate promotional approaches and techniques and of the management issues surrounding each of them. No simple categorisation of promotional approaches is possible but, for ease of reference, this chapter divides them into nine main types:

- people;
- prospectuses, brochures and flyers;
- other written material;
- the media;
- advertising;
- open evenings and other events;
- promotional videos;
- group promotion;
- other communication techniques.

Before examining each approach in turn, we must remind the reader of the existence of both the internal and external markets. Those who constitute the internal market – for example, staff, governors, current pupils and their parents – are the ambassadors of the school in the wider community, that is, in the external market. When considering promotional approaches, the school's first priority must be to ensure that these ambassadors have accurate and positive information to disseminate. Leaders should be confident that there is a consistent message going out about the aims of the school and about the activities which are taking place in order to achieve those aims. This information may be in a visual form – for example, a prospectus, brochure, other publication or pieces of pupils' work – but it is equally likely to be delivered by word of mouth. As well as considering the message which is being delivered, it is very important that there is an awareness of the significance of the delivery method as this can convey hidden messages. We will now deal with each promotional approach in turn.

People

The oldest and still, in many respects, the most powerful means of promoting the school is by word of mouth. The significance of this can be summed up by our belief that every school has a 'school-gate mafia'. This is not a problem for the school as long as it recognises that it has to manage the 'mafia' in the interests of the school. This section is not taking a cynical view of communications by word of mouth but uses that example to demonstrate the power of the word of mouth and the importance of a pro-active approach to managing such communications.

A good way of categorising these oral communications is to think of them as the four Ps:

- Pupils
- Parents
- Professionals
- Public.

Assuming that 'parents' refers to the parents of the current pupils or those who have recently left, the first three of the Ps are part of the internal market. The importance of internal communications with these ambassadors cannot be overestimated. They are perceived by the general public as having an inside view and, therefore, the information which they pass on is perceived to be valid. They should be equipped with the right messages and with high quality materials which reflect the premium product and service being provided by the school. One of the characteristics of the British personality is self deprecation and modesty; this is not always an advantage in marketing terms. More of the American viewpoint – exemplified by 'We are at the best school' – is necessary if positive attitudes and messages are to be conveyed. A central task for school management is to decide how to encourage this type of attitude and pride in the school.

It is not completely true that the first three Ps deal with the internal market as one of them – Professionals – is also part of the external market. These are the headteachers and staff of feeder/partner schools. When faced with a choice of school in the future, parents will often consult the professionals whom they have come to trust and who best know the educational needs of the child. It is expected that fellow teachers will have an accurate view of the schools in the area. If such 'word-of-mouth' communications are to be to your school's advantage, it is important to ensure that all those who work in the feeder/ partner schools have the same accurate information and positive views as the internal ambassadors.

The fourth P – the public – can be a very powerful determinant of the school's image in the community. If the public begin to talk about the school in particularly complimentary or disparaging terms, the message soon spreads. It is important, therefore, to ensure that the message is a positive one.

When schools deal with people in all of these categories, and especially with the external market, the way that the oral communication is transmitted and, more importantly, how it is perceived can be vital to the marketing effort. When answering the telephone and dealing with requests to talk to the headteacher, replies such as 'I don't know where the head is. He/she is always wandering around somewhere' could be replaced with 'The headteacher is with pupils at this moment and always gives priority to pupil learning. Can he/she ring you back later?' This may have a better communication effect in terms of the school's reputation.

The way that other oral presentations and interactions at parents' meetings, open days and other events are carried out is significant in forming an impression of the school. This important area should not be ignored. The focus should not only be on written communications to the detriment of oral communications.

Exercise 10.1 focuses on the role of people in delivering the marketing message.

Prospectuses, brochures and flyers

Although many people use the terms interchangeably, there is a difference between a prospectus and a brochure. While *a prospectus* is obviously designed to be an attractive promotional document, in the case of maintained schools in England and Wales, it must also comply with the statutory requirements as set out by the DfEE. A maintained school *must* have such a prospectus but decisions can then be made about whether to have other material for either promotion or information. An example of such material would be *a brochure* which can be a much shorter document designed to encourage prospective parents to contact the school. Similarly, *flyers* – flat or folded single sheets of information – can attract potential clients to the school in a very cost-effective way. Each of these documents is described in more detail below and the characteristics of good document design which can be applied by the reader are also outlined.

Prospectuses

First impressions are important and a large number of secondary schools have developed high quality, glossy prospectuses, although there is less evidence of this in the primary sector where resources are more constrained and the potential market is smaller. In the secondary sector, such publications are designed to impress so they focus on the strong points of the schools – for example, the extensive playing fields, the well equipped laboratories and the attentive pupils. There is usually reference to a caring community and the development of the full potential of every pupil. There can be hidden messages conveyed through visual images – for example, the ex-grammar school which reminds clients of its 'traditional' values by giving prominence to the school crest and motto. Independent schools have long practised the art of summing up a great many messages in one photograph. Two pupils, a boy and girl in traditional uniform, textbooks under the arm, standing in front of the school chapel would represent the school as follows:

- uniform = standards and discipline
- textbooks = academic standards and study
- the chapel = traditional values and approaches
- a boy and a girl = a mixed school.

All these messages can be conveyed in one photograph. If the prospectus is to attract clients, the text and graphics should reflect the expectations of the clients in that particular school's community (as identified through market research).

It is important to achieve a balance between the quality of presentation and the information being transmitted. If the document is too glossy and superficial some parents may ask what is missing or being covered up. Under a delegated budgetary system, it may raise questions about money being better spent on pupils and not being wasted! However, the counter-argument is that, because of formula funding, if the prospectus brings in an extra ten pupils (yielding £12 000 to £25 000) and costs the school £2000, then it could be considered worthwhile and cost-effective.

As was mentioned earlier, there is a legal obligation for all maintained schools in England and Wales to have a prospectus – a parents' handbook which sets out basic information about the school such as the name of the head and chair of governors, the curriculum, the charging policy and the uniform requirements. The complete requirements for a school prospectus are set out by the Department for Education and Employment; these are updated on a regular basis and so it is important that it is the latest document that is checked.

It is important for the school to ensure that the information in the prospectus is accurate despite the fact that it may change quite frequently. There are various ways of achieving this accuracy.

1 The school can regularly reprint and recirculate a highly professional, glossy publication that covers the legal requirements but refers parents to more detailed documentation in the school which amplifies the basic information provided.
2 The school can produce a high quality folder with similarly high quality individual information sheets which fit inside it. While a long print run may be used for the folder the inserts can be changed each year. This avoids some of the obvious drawbacks of the high cost related to the possibly quite minor amendments about which the parents have to be informed.
3 The school can produce a cheaper publication on the school premises (or at the local secondary school) using in-house desktop publishing facilities. This can give reasonable quality at a lower price than using a commercial typesetter and printer.

The school can produce information sheets for other purposes too. These will provide details which either: change frequently, such as staff lists, or only apply to certain groups, such as option details. The advantage of this approach is that the sheets can be used separately for their specific purpose or be combined together to form the last section of the prospectus. Although they are not an integral part of the prospectus or brochure it is important that each sheet is properly presented. Tenth-generation photocopies will do nothing to enhance a school's reputation.

Key points in prospectus design

There are many management considerations which the school has to bear in mind when undertaking the production of a prospectus. A number of specific points are listed below.

1 *Decide on the purpose – marketing, reference or both?* Is the prospectus going to include everything or is more detail going to be found in other documents in the school? Is it to be a handbook which acts as a complete reference document or is it to be a focused document with the central aim of projecting the right image for the school? There is the danger of trying to do too many things in the prospectus so that it becomes cluttered and loses its impact.
2 *There should be a simple, eye-catching and tasteful cover.* It is especially important to try out prospective designs on clients to get their opinion on what is effective.
3 *Decide on the key issues in the prospectus.* State the school's mission near the beginning and then reinforce key words from the mission statement in the various sections. If a sense of purpose and a clear message are to be

communicated, readers need to know straight away what the school stands for. It is very important, therefore, that the mission statement is at the beginning. Bad prospectus design results in the reader having to turn four or five pages to find this information.

4 *Decide on the strengths to put across.* This can be done either explicitly by describing them in the written text or implicitly – for example, by including key photographs. The right photograph can be worth a thousand words; in the earlier case from an independent school, the picture in front of the chapel is an example of this. Similarly, messages are conveyed by lists such as those which contain staff qualifications.

5 *Structure it clearly.* Bold headings and concise text broken up by appropriate photographs or charts would obviously be better than columns of dense text.

6 *Keep the reader in mind.* The danger of teachers preparing a prospectus is that they may use language and jargon that is common to them but not so clearly understood by the wider community. It is important to realise that several different types of audience displaying different levels of understanding of the educational world will read the document. It must be written in clear straightforward language which will be easily understood by these different readers – not an easy task but one that is critical to the success of the document. A group of parents and pupils can assist here.

7 *Make it easy to read.* Following on from the point above, it is worth comparing an income tax form and an application form for a competition in a tabloid newspaper. The former will be far less comprehensible. We do not necessarily advocate adopting the latter's style but it does make the point. Those producing the material should focus on four factors: the length of the sentences or paragraphs, the reading age and educational knowledge of the reader, the use of appropriate language and the use of both attractive and suitable font sizes. There should be a friendly welcoming style which leaves the reader wanting to know more.

8 *Use high quality illustrations.* Whether they are photographs or line drawings, illustrations are not just there to fill up space but to make the document visually exciting and interesting, to convey messages and, above all, to keep the clients reading and looking! It is quite likely that there will be a big difference between the type of illustrations which are used to market the different phases of education. A primary school prospectus may include pupils' line drawings depicting aspects of school life whereas this message would be conveyed by photographs for a secondary school.

9 *Do not make the prospectus too long.* Not only does this add to the expense, but effectiveness is often lost after the first few pages. It is important to establish ideas and information in a precise and concise way and not to have the reader overcome by volume. National curriculum documentation should not be used as a model!

10 *Do not normally include material which dates.* For most schools it is too costly to reset the prospectus completely each year. Such information can be provided as an insert or as loose sheets inside the back cover.

11 *Ensure that there is a prominent display of how to contact the school.* We have come across several prospectuses with blank back covers! While this is an obvious waste of space it also throws away an opportunity to make the most of the back page. The back page is the perfect spot for a map of where to find the school, its address and telephone number and who to contact. Thus the most important information concerning how to follow up the initial interest aroused by the prospectus comes at the appropriate place and is prominently displayed if the prospectus is left on a table.

12 *Ensure that the prospectus has a professional appearance.* Education has, traditionally, been undersold. If schools believe that they deliver quality in educational terms, then they should represent that quality in other activities. Some schools deliberately go in for marketing acts of self deprecation by producing poorly printed information. The business that has an income of up to £4 million should not represent itself as an amateurish enterprise; this implies that the school does not take itself or, more importantly, its clients seriously and so produces second-class materials.

There is no identikit perfect prospectus or structure that we could recommend, nor would we want to do so. Each school must use an approach which best suits its individual needs and which appeals to the clients in the area. We suggest that, in evaluating prospectuses, readers ensure that the statutory information is included and that the points listed above are applied.

Brochures

Rather than being a totally different publication in terms of content, the brochure can be a shortened version of the prospectus. It is used for publicity purposes where more general information is needed for a wider audience. Resource constraints have caused many schools to rely on the use of a comprehensive prospectus or a limited flyer as promotional literature but an increasing number are producing brochures containing a message from the headteacher along with some photographs and text which show the key features of the school.

Flyers

These are usually double-sided folded sheets of A3 or A4 paper. They act as introductory leaflets or tasters and are used to cover a wider geographical area or a wider range of clients than the prospectus or brochure. Very often a flyer can be of immense value if it gives the name and type of school and some basic information including a map of the school's location and who to contact. Flyers are obviously relatively cheap to produce and can be taken to local estate agents, removal firms and so on for distribution with their normal literature. This will create an awareness of where the school is and what it does so that those whose interest is aroused can telephone the school for the full prospectus. Some schools not only put the name of the headteacher and the school telephone number but also two or three current parents (such as members of the PTA) who are prepared to speak to prospective parents. It is obviously important to select the parents carefully!

A promotional flyer should:

- be eye-catching and visually pleasing;
- feature the school's name prominently;
- include a contact address and map;
- articulate the mission and strengths of the school;
- use suitable vocabulary;
- use good illustrations.

As well as cost considerations, it is likely that the overall quality of the flyer will be partly dependent on what other schools in the area are producing. Increasingly, in the secondary sector, this means full colour photographs and a glossy finish.

The flyer used by one of our international contacts – Surfside Primary School in Australia – is shown in Fig 10.1 and the flyer of a secondary school in the UK – Hounslow Manor School – is shown in Fig 10.2.

Distribution of prospectuses, brochures and flyers

There is no point in producing this material unless someone is going to read it! So what are the most effective ways of bringing the documentation to the eyes of the client or prospective client?

We said earlier that governors, staff, pupils and parents are all ambassadors of the school but they can only help if they realise that they are ambassadors and if they are kept informed. Obviously, existing governors and staff need to have an up-to-date prospectus if they are to represent the school. Prospective parents will also need to be given a copy. Existing parents will receive an initial copy when their children join the school and may only require a second copy when significant changes have been made. When deciding where to place copies, the following list may act as a useful reference. Each school will have to decide whether it is full prospectuses or shorter brochures and flyers which are distributed in each case. If you discover that your school has been recommended by one of these organisations, make sure that you thank the person responsible.

1 *Nursery, primary or middle schools.* The transfer of pupils from one phase of education to the next provides the key recruitment point. Headteachers and

staff of these schools should be kept up to date about your school and supplied with all the necessary prospectuses and other material. This is obviously easier if the school deals with a limited number of feeder/partner schools but regular communication, co-operation and information should be top priorities in the marketing effort as the staff of these schools are often asked about a suitable school by parents of pupils at the age of transfer. If such staff have several copies of a good quality prospectus, it can convey positive messages about your school at this critical decision time.

2 *Public libraries.* Most libraries now have an area where leaflets about local organisations or activities are displayed. The school's literature should feature in this section but it is also worth asking whether the staff are interested in having a copy of your school's prospectus in the reference section. Again this becomes a source of information to prospective parents making a choice about a school.

3 *Information centres.* Many towns have information centres and it is important that they know about your school and have the relevant literature in case new parents to the area ask for help.

4 *Citizens' Advice Bureaux.* These bureaux can be a significant contact point for parents who are new to an area and who want information about local schools. They obviously need a stock of prospectuses and flyers to distribute as and when appropriate. For a list of the bureaux in your area, you should write to the Citizens' Advice Bureaux, National Headquarters, Myddleton House, 105–123 Pentonville Road, London, N1.

5 *Estate agents and removal firms.* Parents moving into an area will, in the first instance, contact estate agents for house details. If, at the same time, the agent can send them literature about local schools in the form of a flyer, then the initial contact will be made. The parents can then obtain information from the flyer and contact the school to request further details. While it may be too expensive to provide the agent with several hundred copies of the full prospectus, the provision of the same number of single A4 sheets or flyers is not. The estate agent could also be provided with a limited number of prospectuses to give out on request. It is important to maintain personal contacts with the agency staff, not only to keep them regularly supplied with the school's literature, but also to ensure that they themselves transmit positive messages about the school. It is also worth noting that some removal firms provide packs of information about an area and it would be worth checking whether they include information about local schools.

6 *Doctors' and dentists' waiting rooms, clinics, hairdressers.* There are a number of places where we sit and wait – doctors, dentists, health clinics, hospital outpatients' departments, solicitors' offices. Instead of people being faced with the prospect of reading a six-month-old copy of *Woman's Own* or *Car Mechanics*, up-to-date information about your school could be placed in these areas. This will convey a picture of your school as it currently operates and is a sound marketing approach within the local community. At the

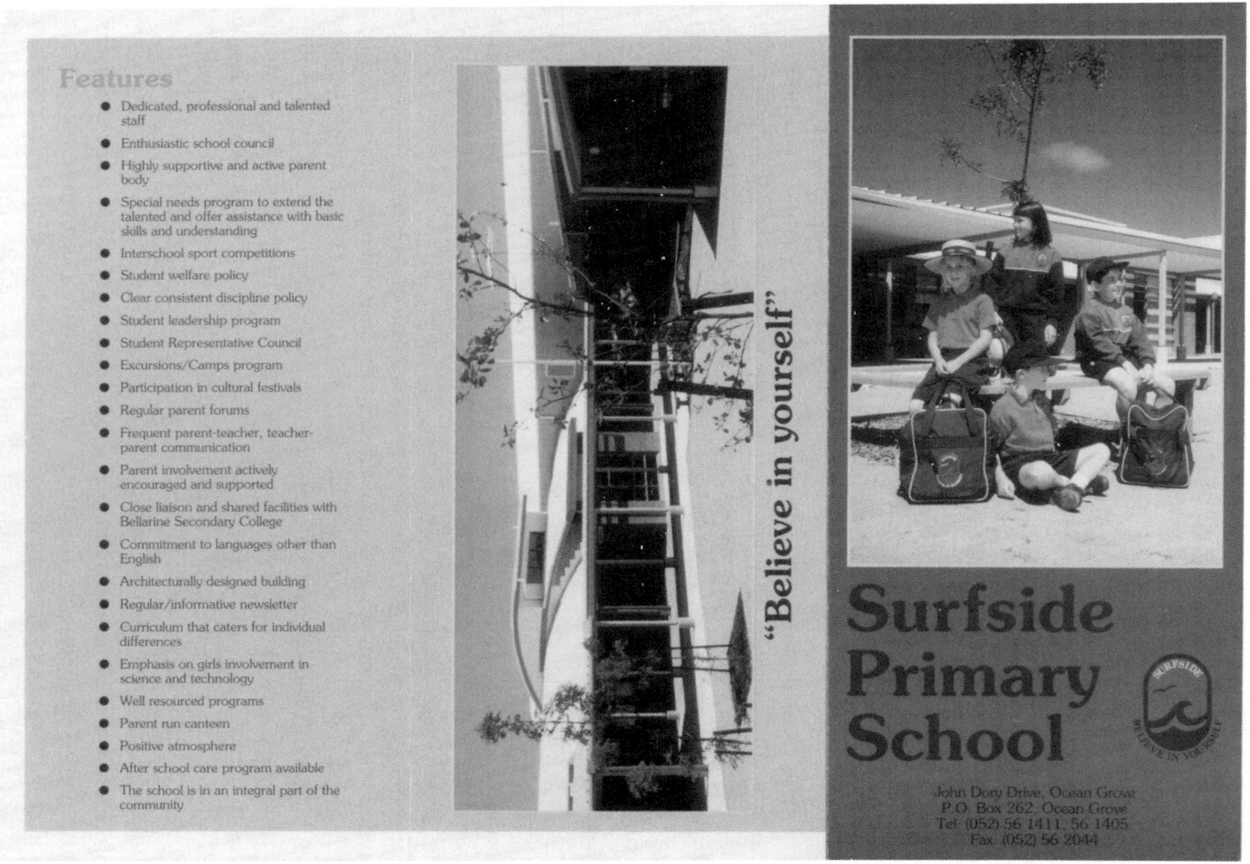

Features

- Dedicated, professional and talented staff
- Enthusiastic school council
- Highly supportive and active parent body
- Special needs program to extend the talented and offer assistance with basic skills and understanding
- Interschool sport competitions
- Student welfare policy
- Clear consistent discipline policy
- Student leadership program
- Student Representative Council
- Excursions/Camps program
- Participation in cultural festivals
- Regular parent forums
- Frequent parent-teacher, teacher-parent communication
- Parent involvement actively encouraged and supported
- Close liaison and shared facilities with Bellarine Secondary College
- Commitment to languages other than English
- Architecturally designed building
- Regular/informative newsletter
- Curriculum that caters for individual differences
- Emphasis on girls involvement in science and technology
- Well resourced programs
- Parent run canteen
- Positive atmosphere
- After school care program available
- The school is in an integral part of the community

"Believe in yourself"

Surfside Primary School

Surfside
Believe in yourself

John Dory Drive, Ocean Grove
P.O. Box 262, Ocean Grove
Tel: (052) 56 1411, 56 1405
Fax: (052) 56 2044

Fig 10.1 Flyer for Surfside Primary School

Surfside Primary School

History

The Victorian Ministry of Education in September 1990 initiated the development and planning of a new school in Ocean Grove.

In November, the New School Planning Committee was formed comprising prospective parents, community representatives and Ministry personnel with the charter of planning the development and building of the school. This work culminated in the school's opening in January 1992 based at the Ocean Grove Primary School site. In May 1993 the staff and pupils moved to the new building in John Dory Drive.

From the beginning the planning has emphasised the value of strong community involvement, an enthusiastic and professional approach to education and the establishment of a stimulating and challenging environment for everyone involved. These qualities are constantly focused on, so as to provide the best possible primary school education for our children.

Vision

Mission Statement

This statement was developed by students, parents and staff to provide a basis for our planning and operation.

At Surfside we have a commitment to:

- a caring and safe atmosphere which values emotional, social and academic development.
- a team approach where the opinions of students, teachers and parents are listened to and valued.
- a stimulating environment promoting a variety of teaching and learning styles emphasising individual effort and improvement.
- an open, welcoming and trusting environment
- high expectations of everyone.
- well resourced programs and school facilities
- a planned future with everyone working towards shared goals
- fun, excitement, risk taking and creativity.

Curriculum

Sequential Preparatory to Year 6 course to cater for all students.

Curriculum areas include:

- ■ Sport
- ■ Music
- ■ Science
- ■ Computers
- ■ Arts/Drama
- ■ Library
- ■ Technology
- ■ Swimming
- ■ Mathematics
- ■ Camping/Excursion Program
- ■ Health & Physical Education
- ■ English Language Studies
- ■ Personal Development
- ■ Studies of Society and Environment
- ■ Languages other than English

Facilities

Our excellent facilities include:

- ▲ Art Room
- ▲ Resource Centre (Library)
- ▲ Gymnasium & change rooms
- ▲ Canteen
- ▲ Interview Rooms
- ▲ Health Centre
- ▲ Music Room
- ▲ Netball Courts (indoor & outdoor)
- ▲ Basketball Courts (indoor & outdoor)
- ▲ Sports Ovals
- ▲ Meeting Rooms
- ▲ Lounge
- ▲ Adventure Playground
- ▲ Bicycle storage
- ▲ Paved Amphitheatre
- ▲ Full security system
- ▲ Extensive grassed playground
- ▲ Indoor amenities

Classrooms

All have –

- ✦ individual gas heating
- ✦ wet areas
- ✦ ceiling fans
- ✦ teacher offices
- ✦ small work rooms
- ✦ ample storage for bike helmets/bags/coats
- ✦ outside courtyards
- ✦ northerly aspect
- ✦ a bright and pleasant environment
- ✦ carpet

Fig 10.1 continued

Courses Offered.....

The school is organised into Faculties:

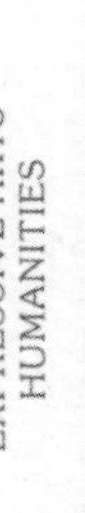

MATHS SCIENCE
CREATIVE ARTS
EXPRESSIVE ARTS
HUMANITIES

We offer the following courses at GCSE/A-Level:

Art	Geography
Biology	German
CDT	Graphical Communication
Chemistry	History
Computer Studies	Maths
Drama	Music
Economics	Physics
Electronics	Religious Studies
English Language	Spanish
English Literature	Technology
French	Theatre Studies

Facilities......

* Excellent special needs provision.
* Two gymnasia and an excellent Sports Hall.
* Three computer networks (a total of over 120 computers amongst the departments.)
* Two fully-equipped Business Studies rooms.
* Several Art studios and a ceramics room.
* Excellent facilities for Technology.

HOUNSLOW MANOR SCHOOL

Prince Regent Road,
Hounslow,
Middlesex. TW3 1NE

Tel: 081-572 4461

Fig 10.2 Flyer for Hounslow Manor School

Message from Roger Shortt

Headteacher......

I believe that young people have a limitless potential for growth and development. It is our intention to ensure that our pupils are given the opportunities in which they may reach the highest levels of achievement in all aspects of their education. We recognise that we are helping young people prepare themselves for adult life in the 21st century and that we are providing them with the 'keys' to further and higher education. We have many outstanding pupils at our school and for us 'the sky's the limit'. This leaflet will give you a brief glimpse of our school; I know you will be impressed.

Hounslow Manor

Hounslow Manor is situated in the centre of Hounslow within three minutes walk of the Bus Station and the Piccadilly Line. There has been a school on this site for over sixty years.

Hounslow Manor was formed in 1968 when the Borough had a major educational re-organisation. It is a school of 800 pupils, housed on a single site.

Our Strengths include:

* A friendly and caring school.
* Dedicated, well-qualified teachers.
* Work experience for all pupils in the upper school.
* Field work and educational trips at home and abroad.
* Sporting activities for all.
* A wide range of A-Level subjects.

Education at its best

Fig 10.2 continued

hairdressers there is the opportunity to engage in conversation about schools, so a positive image for your own school can be reinforced by the local grapevine as well as by the documentation.

7 *Local business firms.* Local commercial and industrial firms should, wherever possible, be given up-to-date copies of the school prospectus and other information. This can be sent to the person who deals with school–industry links and also to the personnel department which deals with relocated staff. In this way, the school may recruit more pupils but, more importantly, it will enhance its image so that industry links, teacher placements and pupils' job opportunities are improved. There may even be opportunities for sponsorship of the school's activities or its publicity materials.

8 *Local press and media.* Local newspapers and local radio need to be kept supplied with regular news information about the school, a point which is developed later in this chapter. In the first instance, they need to have reference material about the school and this can be obtained from the prospectus. The school should therefore ensure that an up-to-date copy is supplied to all local newspapers (including the 'free' ones) and radio stations.

Other written material

If the school has spent a great deal of time and effort producing a high quality prospectus it needs to ensure that the rest of its written material reflects that quality approach. We have seen some professionally produced prospectuses which have inserts in the back that have been run off on duplicators of indifferent quality. This destroys the quality impression that has initially been created. The school must therefore display a quality approach in all its material.

Corporate identity

Most schools have some sort of logo, crest or other symbol of corporate identity. This enables their documentation to be distinguished from others and helps to give a sense of 'belonging' to the members of the school. Care should be taken to ensure that the symbol is used in a consistent way every time. For example, it should feature on headed notepaper but should also appear somewhere, perhaps in a smaller form, on other printed materials. The logo of Broughton Junior School is shown in Fig 10.3. As well as being used on its sweatshirts, this logo is used on its stationery, publicity materials, records of achievement and so on. Large corporations in the business world spend a great deal of money on designing a corporate logo which conveys the right image and, above all, assists in recognisability of the firm and its product. It is worth reflecting that they see great value in displaying a professionally designed, consistent image. Schools are not businesses but they do need to display some of the same corporate attributes.

Headteacher Mr P K Hargrave

Fig 10.3 The logo of Broughton Junior School and an example of one of its many uses

General correspondence

All letters need to be produced on the school notepaper using a standard display system without any mistakes. The tone should be courteous and problem-solving and not aggressive. This is easy to achieve when letters are produced for the senior management team by staff in the general office but it does require some effort to ensure that staff throughout the school use the same approach.

Information for job applicants

When information sheets are compiled for prospective job applicants they often comprise a collection of sheets produced by different people at different times. This can result in a lack of consistency which can give negative messages about the school and its organisation. There will probably be a covering letter, but all other sheets such as those which describe the school and those which focus on the particular post should be displayed in a similar style. When advertising a post, it is important to have the materials ready for distribution otherwise prospective candidates are given the impression that the school is disorganised and they are annoyed at not having many days to complete their applications.

Newsletters

One of the minor, but recurring, complaints about schools is that they do not always communicate effectively with parents and other clients. A newsletter is a popular way of attempting to bridge the gap between home and school. Unfortunately, there is still a lot of criticism about length, layout, frequency and content, even when the school has spent a lot of time and money on the production of the newsletter. Market research should reveal information about the clients' preferences with regard to format that will enable the school to negate these criticisms and produce a properly targeted newsletter. Sometimes there may be a preference for an infrequent school newsletter but more regular year group sheets. Whatever the case, when preparing a newsletter it would seem sensible to bear in mind the following points:

- *It should not be not too long.* There is a tendency to stop reading after a few pages. One or two sides may be ideal because this avoids high costs and possible collation problems.
- *It should be frequent enough to keep parents informed about activities but not so frequent as to become too ordinary.*
- *It must be easy to read.* As with all written communications, this refers to the language and the layout.
- *There should be an interesting layout* – broken up by lists and diagrams.
- *It is useful to apply some of the rules for prospectus design* from earlier in this chapter.

While it may be a good idea to produce a newsletter and send it out with the pupils acting as the deliverers, most teachers know that there is no guarantee that it will ever reach home! Using a return slip which is signed by parents can be of great value in checking on delivery but can be frustrating for class teachers who have to collect the slips. A better solution may be to send home written communications such as newsletters on the same day each week so that parents can be advised to ask that night for them. If the pupils and their friends have been involved in developing the newsletter and if they feel that it is of value, then they are more likely to deliver it. This is another example of the importance of communicating to the internal market first.

Secondary school curriculum choice and option booklets

Some schools take little care over information which they prepare for their existing pupils and for their parents. This attitude ignores the significance of the internal market. If it is an option booklet which is being produced, the subject staff must view the activity as one by which they are marketing their subjects to the pupils. Even where subjects are compulsory, it is important for pupils to see them projected in a positive way so that they feel that a high quality product is going to be delivered. Teachers need to display a serious professional approach when dealing with this aspect of marketing if they expect a similar attitude from the pupils when they undertake the subject. Although most of the potential pupils are within the school, it may be that a school attracts pupils from outside because of the way in which it promotes its curriculum and option structure – for example at the end of Key Stage 3. There is certainly considerable potential for recruitment from outside the school at the end of Key Stage 4. Schools will be in competition, not only with neighbouring schools, but also with sixth form colleges and colleges of further education so marketing should also be aimed at retaining the existing Year 11 pupils. These competitors may be promoting a wider range of services and products than a school can provide so it is important to have done the market research and to put across a strong message which reflects client expectations.

School reports/Records of achievement

A school report is one item of information that all parents will read and most will keep! The opportunity should not be lost therefore to produce a document which enhances the school's image and reputation. This means that it must convey useful information, rather than platitudes or brief words of condemnation. Staff should understand the importance of consistency of approach when compiling reports, especially if grades are used. It is obviously important that reports should be free of spelling mistakes and grammatical errors and senior staff should establish monitoring systems in order to ensure that this objective is achieved. Adequate time should be set aside for this important means of communicating with the clients.

Letters and information packs about school visits

Letters form one of the most common communications between the home and the school. However, as they are often produced by a variety of teachers, the standard of presentation and clarity of explanation can vary considerably. There is an obvious need for senior management to monitor these to ensure that the highest communication standards are being met. Many pupils keep their programmes as souvenirs of school trips or add them to scrapbooks or project work so a professional image is projected beyond the duration of the visit.

Figure 10.4 shows the programme prepared by Weaver County Primary School which suggests that the visit will be of a high quality and that pupils' welfare has been given priority.

Annual report to parents

The quality of these varies enormously from those which are dry official documents to those which give an interesting account of the school's activities. While the governors in England and Wales must meet the requirements of the 1986 Education Act, the production of the document should not be seen as a chore but more as an opportunity to convey information and to promote a positive image about the school.

When looking at all the written material which the school sends out the central factor is quality and, above all, consistent quality. Good examples in one area of activity can be undone by poor presentation in another. Leaders of schools should strive to ensure that different items sent out by different people in the school reflect that quality and create a positive impression of the school. The simple rules of clear language, easy to read, good display and so on will remain just rules unless there is that overriding commitment to quality.

The media

Local and national media can be very significant in conveying messages, whether deliberately or accidentally. Schools must constantly be aware of this power, both in their direct dealings with the media and in their general day-to-day activities. Free publicity is very useful – if it is of the right kind! The school can build the use of media messages into its promotional strategies and can set up systems which will minimise the damage if any adverse messages reach the media concerning the school.

Although the full range of media is potentially available to schools, the types vary in their significance and in the way in which they might be used. National or regional television is prohibitively expensive as an advertising medium but it could be possible to have the school featured in a programme. This is only likely to occur if the school has achieved something unusual (preferably positive!) which is of interest to the public at large. Recent experiments in local television may lead to a more appropriate means of communicating a school's purpose and activities to the immediate community.

There is a similar pattern with other forms of media. Local radio may be more willing than national channels to feature the school in its programmes and the advertising slots will be more cost-effective because they will be cheaper and are more likely to reach the target clients. National newspapers are only likely to feature schools which have achieved 'firsts' of public interest or have achieved notoriety for some reason. On the other hand, the local press may be very willing to print material about a school. Most of the rest of this section applies to relations with the local press but could, if the circumstances arose, be applied to the other media.

We believe that there are two types of news – the good and the bad – and that, therefore, two approaches and sets of procedures are required. While it may be desirable to designate a member of staff who will liaise with the press on general matters, we believe that, when a problem arises and the media takes an interest, then all dealings must be with the head or a nominated deputy. This person should be able to handle the situation sensitively because he or she has an overview of the issues and has experience in relating to the external environment in which the school exists.

It is important to develop a whole school policy for dealing with the good and the bad news and to communicate that policy by producing guidance for staff on all aspects of media links. Each partner in the school's activities – whether it is a member of staff, governor, pupil or parent – will then be aware of the possibilities and procedures. This will avoid a sparsity of coverage or, on the other hand, duplication of material and effort. The paragraphs which follow look at possible elements of a policy and set of procedures, using a simple division into the Who?, Why?, What?, When? of media links. (We have not attempted to give a lot of detail about the operational aspects of the policy here but we recommend to the reader *Public Relations and Marketing for Schools* by Tim Devlin and Brian Knight (Longman, 1990) which gives excellent coverage of this area. This was one of the first books in the field but it is still very useful.

1 *Who?* As indicated earlier, we believe that a policy should nominate those responsible for direct links with the media. In the case of bad news, this should be the head, deputy or chair of governors. It should be made clear to all staff that, under no circumstances, do they make comments on behalf of the school, however innocent the question seems. At critical times it is important that a consistent balanced view is expressed and that the press are not given the opportunity to exploit a number of ill thought-out responses. It is always worth remembering that newspapers exist to sell

PROGRAMME

YEAR 6 - VISIT TO YORK

18 - 22 MARCH 1996

Monday 18 March	9.00am	Depart Nantwich Eden Camp, Malton Lunch in Mess Hut
	5.30pm approx.	Arrive York
Tuesday 19 March	10.00am 10.15 12.30 pm pm	National Railway Museum Magicians Road Lunch in Study Coach N.R.M.
Wednesday 20 March	10.00am	York Minster Lunch at York Minster
	1.00pm 2.30	Jorvik Centre The Arc
Thursday 21 March	10.00am	Museum of Automata Lunch at Museum of Automata
	2.00pm	Castle Museum
Friday 22 March	am	City tour by bus
	12 noon 3.00pm approx.	Depart York for Nantwich Arrive back at school

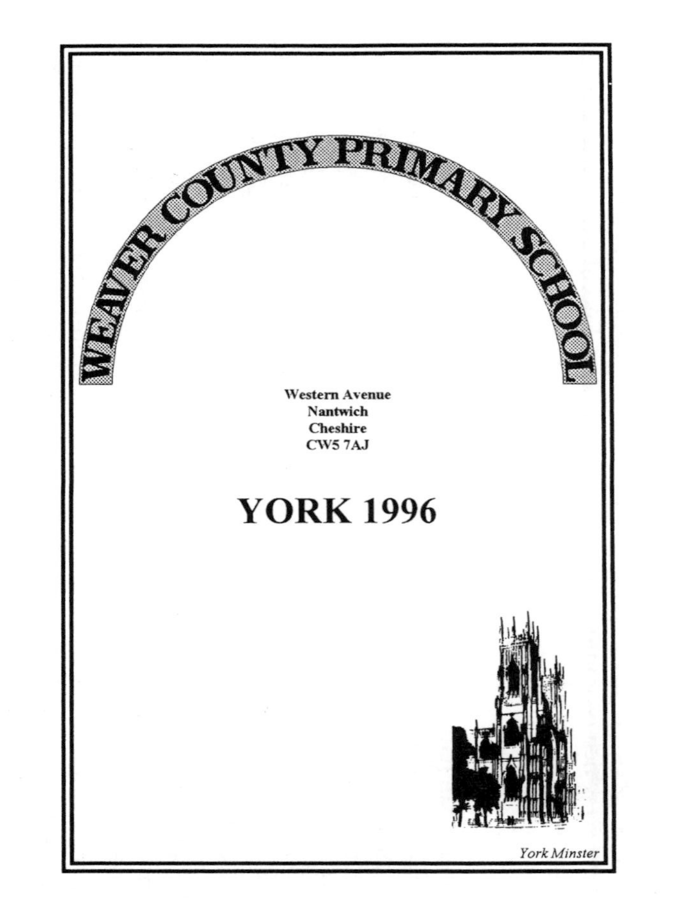

Fig 10.4 Programme from Weaver County Primary School

Wheatlands Lodge
78-85 Scarcroft Road
York
North Yorkshire
Y02 1DB

Tel: 01904 654318

Page 1

CHECK LIST OF ITEMS FOR VISIT TO YORK

18 MARCH - 22 MARCH 1996

- Waterproof coat
- Cagoule
- Strong shoes
- Indoor shoes - trainers
- Slippers
- Toilet requirements and towel
- Night clothes
- Indoor clothes/Outdoor clothes)
  Socks/shirts/sweaters/underwear/trousers
- Camera (own responsibility)
- Plastic bag for dirty clothes

Fig 10.4 continued

copies and not necessarily to protect the reputation of schools! In the case of good news, different staff may be chosen to deal with the press. One aspect of this role is to ensure that there is coverage of a range of the school's activities to reflect the diversity of the educational experience and to appeal to a wide range of clients.

2 *Why?* The main reason for a media policy is to ensure a co-ordinated approach, enabling consistent, positive information to be transmitted to the media. A named person can build the links, co-ordinate press releases and ensure exposure by utilising personal links and contacts. Thus the publication of good news can, like any other marketing strategy, enhance the school's reputation, advertise its events, recruit more pupils and generate resources in other ways. If relationships are good, then when something goes wrong in the school, the media are more likely to take a sympathetic or supportive line than to seek exaggerated headlines.

3 *What?* Copy about the school's past or future activities can be supplied to the media. This should be relatively concise and should be compiled with some understanding of what will gain and retain the readers' interest. It is also possible for staff and pupils to be interviewed by journalists or presenters, but care should be taken here because the school has little control over what is published. There have been several examples nationally in which this type of relationship has been to the school's detriment.

   The following list gives an idea of the topics which tend to be of interest to the public and hence to the media:

   - sporting achievements;
   - academic achievements;
   - new developments such as the increased use of technology or joint community use of the premises;
   - open days or evenings;
   - competition successes;
   - individuals' involvement in unusual activities;
   - visits and visitors, especially where overseas links are involved;
   - community and charity involvement.

4 *When?* The role of the person who liaises with the media is to ensure that there is regular coverage of the school in the local media without submitting so much material that there is overkill. Excessive publicity can give the impression that the school is only interested in activities which are newsworthy or that it is short of pupils. It is obviously important to time publicity to coincide with school events and with the time at which choices of school are made by parents.

Advertising

Most of the indirect forms of advertising have been discussed in the preceding sections. As well as these indirect forms, many more schools are now turning to direct 'paid for' advertising in order to publicise their existence and their activities. Formal advertising may be in local newspapers or on local radio (television is usually prohibitively expensive and covers too wide an area) or by the use of notices at strategic spots in the local community or in local magazines or newsletters. Schools already undertake a considerable amount of advertising but the scope has widened recently. The following options are appropriate for school advertising:

1 *Staff vacancies.* This is the traditional form of advertising in which schools have been involved. They have used the national educational press such as the *Times Educational Supplement*, the *Education Guardian* or the local press. Now that schools, rather than LEAs, are bearing the cost of these advertisements, they are identifying the target group more carefully and considering the cost-effectiveness of the various newspapers and journals. If it is felt that a suitable candidate will be based locally – for example, for a temporary post – then the local press can be used. On the other hand, when attempting to attract a high quality field for a senior post, the school should prepare an advertisement which gives a view of the school – in words, through use of the logo, or both – rather than using the LEA general format. It is important to remember that the advertisement is not just about recruiting a member of staff but also about promoting the image and reputation of the school. There are certain legal requirements to bear in mind when deciding on the format of an advertisement and how widely to advertise a post. These should be checked carefully.
2 *School events.* The advertising of school plays, summer fairs and other events helps to make the individual event viable but is also a wonderful opportunity to attract people inside the school and to display the work of the school to the wider group of clients. Local newspapers, radio, posters, flyers and so on are all methods that would be used here. Care is needed if the event causes extra traffic and parking problems for the school's neighbours otherwise there could be a dysfunctional effect on community relations.
3 *Pupil recruitment.* Some schools use extensive advertising to attract new pupils but this has to be done in an ethical and appropriate way. It is common to publicise open days or evenings for prospective parents. The local press and local radio are the best media for this, especially if such an approach is backed up with leaflets for pupils in the feeder/partner primary schools. A variant on this is to advertise specific areas of the school, such as the sixth form, with lists of subject options and past success rates. This approach can be taken when increasing the size of a school across all age groups is not appropriate; instead it may be possible to target specific

year groups in which the school can increase numbers through making existing group sizes more viable without incurring extra staffing costs.

Wherever advertising is used, it is important to remember certain rules:

- The advertisement should be attractive and eye-catching.
- The advertisement should carry the school's name and location quite clearly.
- If an event is being advertised, the date and time should be included and any entrance fee (if appropriate).
- Potential clients should be clear about how to respond, such as the venue for the event or how to contact the school for further details.
- The advertisement should be tasteful and never, even by vague implication, be disparaging of other schools.

With these rules in mind schools should reconsider the use of advertising. If the cost of an advertisement results in a significant increase in the number of parents at an open evening, who then select the school, that cost will be repaid many times over, especially if it is remembered that a new pupil is in the school for up to seven years!

Open evenings and other events

As described in Chapter Seven, research by Bradley (1996) has shown that the opportunity to see the school is one of the most useful sources of information to those who are choosing schools. It gives the chance to convey the ethos and atmosphere which is a deciding factor for so many parents. Although formal open events are often organised for prospective parents, there are many other opportunities to promote the school to a range of clients. Decisions to choose the school or to support it are often made as a result of a series of interactions rather than through attendance at a single event. Furthermore, preliminary decisions are made much earlier than many schools realise and the special events are only used to confirm or reject a choice.

Open days/evenings

These are significant events which can be advertised locally to bring different groups of people into the school. Traditionally open days have been for potential new pupils but they can also be targeted at different segments of the market. As well as open days for new pupils, the school could have a smaller open day targeted at local commerce and industry in which specific aspects of the schools' work can be illustrated and related to their interests and needs in a much more direct way. The same may be true of local residents and neighbours with which the school wishes to improve relations.

School cultural and sporting events

The publicity value of school concerts, plays and successful sporting achievements has long been realised. The school has to ensure that it organises the communication with local press and media to exploit fully the opportunities created. These events also enable the school to invite younger children into the school so that relationships are built up. Secondary schools may find it valuable to allow primary school children to visit in order to use their specialist facilities such as drama studios, sports equipment or laboratories.

Participation in competitions

Like cultural and sporting events, quizzes, design projects and the like can provide opportunities to publicise and promote positive aspects of the life of the school.

PTA and other parent events

These are a very significant way of involving parents in both supporting the school and of creating opportunities for parents to visit the school. By seeing the work of the school and interacting with the staff, parents can have their decision to send their children to that school reinforced and reaffirmed.

Promotional videos

Schools have tended to follow one of two courses in the production of videos:

1 Those made by pupils of the school showing aspects of school life for use with new children about to transfer. These provide a lively view of the school at work and play.
2 Professionally produced videos that can be used with a much wider audience and which usually display a much higher quality of final product.

The problem with the latter is that, while putting across the school's strengths, they can appear to be stage-managed and can be quite expensive. An interesting way to obtain a professional product at a reasonable cost is through the development of a joint project with students of media studies at a local institution of further or higher education.

Group promotion

Many parents of primary-age children may well be influenced in their choice of school not only by the reputation/quality of the primary school but also by the standard and continuity of education which that school can offer in conjunction with subsequent secondary schools. Several areas have developed 'pyramids' or 'families' of partner schools which formally develop this collaboration.

A significant area for development is, therefore, the concept of a group of schools coming together to market a package of education from four to eighteen. Provided that it is honoured, a promise of co-operation and continuity will attract parents and may even persuade some to 'opt in' from the private sector where such continuity is less common. 'Coherence and Progression' may be a good title for a joint promotional brochure!

The flyer used by the Ilkley Pyramid of schools to promote excellence and continuity of education in the area is shown in Fig 10.5.

Other communication techniques

There are many ways in which a school can engage in conveying an image that enhances or detracts from its reputation. Some of these techniques are not always apparent and it may be that the school does not recognise them or their significance because they are taken for granted and not seen as part of the promotion of the school. Several of these methods are discussed below.

School name

This, in itself, can convey an image of the school. It may be that the school wishes to appear to be traditional and long-established, thus it chooses to retain 'Grammar' in its title to build on the earlier reputation although it has become a comprehensive school. In contrast, those schools which have been granted Technology College status are incorporating that into the school's name in order to convey their particular focus on learning. 'Grant-maintained' may have associations with private schooling for some parents, despite the fact that this type of school is a state school funded in a different way. The inclusion of a reference to the community in the name of the school reminds people that this is a community school or college with all that that entails in terms of access. Some schools feel that events in the past have damaged their reputations and a new name can suggest that things have changed. If this strategy is adopted, it is important to follow it up with *real* improvement.

We include here a case study of one of our research schools which changed its name as part of a strategy to change its image in the local community.

Fig 10.5 A flyer from the Ilkley Pyramid of schools

The Ilkley Pyramid of Schools

This Brochure is not about one school but about ten – ten schools which form the **ILKLEY PYRAMID**.

Learning about how things work and developing co-ordination.

First School Pupils prove that learning to play together is just as important as working together.

This guide for parents demonstrates the unique educational opportunity available in this part of Wharfedale. Here, First, Middle and Upper Schools link closely and successfully. Each school represents a separate stage; together all the schools provide a whole coherent educational experience.

Quite simply education is a building process with each layer depending on foundations laid at an earlier stage. **THE ILKLEY PYRAMID PROVIDES NOT ONLY THE FIRMEST FOUNDATION BUT THE FINEST STRUCTURE.**

A study in creative concentration.

'All my own work'? A study in Handicraft concentration.

First Schools

Schools in Addingham and Ilkley admit children to full time education at the beginning of the term in which their fifth birthday occurs, with some part time admissions available. Burley-in-Wharfedale schools admit children in the September following their fourth birthday to a special pre-five class. All children then remain in First Schools until the end of the academic year in which their ninth birthday falls.

All schools follow the National Curriculum in English, Maths, Science, Technology, History and Geography, in addition to Religious Education, P.E., Art, Music, Movement and Games.

The creation of a happy working environment is our first aim, and all children are encouraged to be aware of their surroundings, and to contribute in every possible way.

Good education is not only about healthy minds but about healthy bodies as well – and the pleasures that can be derived from a variety of sporting opportunities.

Parents are encouraged to contribute by involvement in the classrooms, through PTA activities, and by serving as Governors.

Middle Schools

The spirit of cooperation and 'working together' creates the link through to the Middle Schools and while the National Curriculum is, of course, still followed, the flexibility of the time table encourages all children to develop an enquiring mind and a high level of self-esteem.

A comprehensive Library – for reference, research – or just simply reading

Aesthetic awareness, creativity and a whole host of concepts, skills and knowledge are also acquired as children graduate from class based teaching to being taught by specialist teachers.

Therefore the child gradually takes on more responsibility for his or her own learning, being actively encouraged to set and keep to the highest standards of work, demonstrated through Records of Achievement, so that on transfer to the Upper School children are ready to take advantage of the opportunities for life offered there.

Upper School

Ilkley Grammar School has served the community for over 400 years. It combines the best of the traditional in education with the exciting learning opportunities of a modern, forward-looking comprehensive school. The aim of our experienced and well qualified staff is to develop fully the potential of all pupils and prepare them for adulthood. Sound discipline and a caring atmosphere are the basis of our work.

In the world that is to be their workplace the computer will be a basic tool.

Pupils learn so many things from 'playing shop'.

Fig 10.5 continued

Case Study
Changing the name from Woodhatch to Reigate School

In 1992 this 12–16 school had 400 students and the intake was stable, around 100 students per year group. Clearly, to ensure long-term survival, student numbers had to rise. A major change was planned for September 1993 when the school became an 11–16 school, taking two years of intake at once. This was seen as a major opportunity to boost the roll; the aim was for the size of year groups to approach the planned admission number of 150.

Some sectors of the local community had a favourable impression of the school, while others continued to regard the school as a secondary modern school, which it had once been. Competition for students is considerable in the area with two 11–18 state schools, two other 11–16 schools and two selective independent schools, all accessible to students. When I was appointed head in 1993 there was complete agreement among staff and governors that there would be benefits in a name change in order to attract more students. A decision to do this was taken and a number of other marketing activities were also put into place.

The new name had to be one which related to something which was perceived as positive in the area. In this case the new name was based on an association with the relatively prosperous town of Reigate. There was some media attention including an interview on local radio. The idea was first presented as a press release, encouraging suggestions for a new name and outlining our reasons for making the change. Here we emphasised the positive view that our students now came from a much wider area than Woodhatch, and highlighted the restrictions placed on the school by the continuing notion of catchment areas and of a school with a particular name being only for people in that area. One letter appeared in the press critical of the change but we decided not to respond as we felt that an ongoing debate in the local paper would not benefit the school.

A number of existing conditions – for example, the students' positive attitudes to learning and the school's pleasant internal appearance (resulting from extensive investment in carpeting, curtaining and notice-boards for displaying work of the students) – led us to believe that if we could get people to come and look at our school, we could attract more students. Although refurbishing was expensive, we have since discovered that adults who came to evening classes in the school took out messages of change and improvement. The students already in the school saw this as an investment in them, making their lives more comfortable, which gave a further marketing lift to the school as they told people about the changes.

Other costs to be considered in specifically changing the name were:

- a new prospectus and brochures;
- a new school sign;
- the repainting of the school minibus;
- changes to school pullovers;
- new rubber stamps;
- labels to cover old name in textbooks;
- security marking on equipment;
- new headed note paper;
- new display of school name on every noticeboard;
- school awards, for example, cups and certificates.

These came to less than £1000 – less than the value of one extra student!

The name change was to be the catalyst for getting people interested. A4 glossy brochures with the new name were distributed to primary school children, inviting them to the open evening. We wanted to stimulate interest and make people want to come and look – we had to make sure they were not disappointed. The name was immediately used by the students; in fact I remember watching a school football match at the start of the term and hearing shouts of 'Come on Reigate'. The whole package of marketing ideas, including the name change, has been tremendously successful. The school is now half-way through a £2.5 million building programme which will allow its roll to increase to 1000 students.

John Cain
Headteacher, Reigate School

Distinctive uniform

This can be a 'double-edged sword'. If the uniform displays a high quality image, it can be a significant advantage. However, if the pupils are causing problems in the local fish and chip shop at lunchtime the advantage may not be so apparent! When we undertook a marketing day in a particular school, one of the problems which the school articulated was concerned with location and uniform. There were three schools in the town: two on the fringes and this school in the centre. The two schools on the edge of town had a similar burgundy uniform while that of the school in question was royal blue. At lunchtime pupils from the central school used the fast-food and sweet shops in the town while those from the outlying schools were unable to reach them. It was not that the children at the central school were any better or worse behaved than those attending schools on the fringes but they were considerably more noticeable if there was any trouble. Problems with misbehaviour in the town could be solved with strategies like shorter lunch breaks but in this case changing the colour of the uniform to burgundy may be more effective! This type of analysis can also be applied to a school bus or minibus. If it is new, clean and the children inside it are well behaved then having the school name on the outside could be a positive advantage. If the opposite is true, then the impact is very detrimental in marketing terms. (Putting a rival school's name on the bus is not very ethical!)

School signs and notices

All too often, when visiting a new school, it is difficult to find it. Tell-tale signs appear, such as a flat roof or railings, but the school sign can be small and overgrown by bushes! A school should be proud to proclaim itself to the community and this should be reflected in the school sign. It should be well designed and constructed and easy to read by those passing the school, including motorists who have not been that way before. Traditionally, schools have been dependent on the LEA for signs and notices but, in the era of delegated finance, schools now find the freedom to design and display their own signs a useful advantage. If a school takes care over the appearance of its sign, there is a suggestion that similar care is taken over other aspects of the school. Furthermore, on schools with a large campus or a split site, a number of signs strategically placed are required.

Once a visitor has found the school, it is not always very easy to find one's way around. Finding the way to the secretary's office via the kitchens is not the best way to start a visit. Schools very often have clear signs from the front gate but not from where the visitor is coming – the car park! It is important that the signs and notices around the school are clear and give adequate information. They should also be welcoming. Our most notorious example, mentioned earlier in the book, is the sign on the school gate 'Parents not allowed beyond this point' – perhaps not the most inspired marketing ploy! Unless they are for very short-term use, signs should be made of robust, wipeable materials. It is a good idea to ask a parent to walk round the school and to comment on the effectiveness of direction signs.

The entrance hall

All schools have cultures which are often reflected in their entrance halls. Some have honours boards and trophy cupboards while others have the 'drapes and driftwood' approach. Whatever the preferred style, the entrance hall should be welcoming, well decorated, with displays of pupils' work and somewhere for the visitor to sit down. The reception area should be next to the general office and have easy and immediate access to it.

The way that people are received and where they are received leave an important impression on them. One of the worst types of entrance hall is where there is a small sliding glass window where the visitor rings a bell, waits, and somebody puts their head through the window and says 'Yes?'! This is usually followed by the visitor asking to speak to a specific person and the window being closed again while the person is found. Meanwhile the visitor is left in the entrance hall, sometimes with the added excitement of being there while the pupils go to break. This example is, unfortunately, all too prevalent. We talked in Chapter Three of a client-orientated culture – this is never more evident than in the way people are initially received. Staff training on how to handle visitors – for example, offering a welcoming 'Good morning, can I help you?' and not leaving them standing alone – can be repaid many times over in terms of enhanced reputation for the school.

Now that schools are more security conscious, there is a need to have a way of identifying visitors. If this is handled sensitively, it can give a positive image of the school as one which cares about the security of its members. If this aspect is handled badly, it can cause visitors to feel unwelcome.

Use of school buildings/premises

There is no doubt that letting out school buildings can be a mixed blessing. Few, if any, events are economic if the income received is set against the fixed costs involved in the wear and tear of the buildings and equipment, rather than just against the marginal costs incurred in putting on the activity. It is a requirement that schools cover the direct costs of lettings; they cannot use the school budget to subsidise any external bodies. Why then should schools be involved in hiring out their premises to different groups in the community?

Allowing different groups in the community to use the building for meetings or courses can have a considerable spin-off in marketing terms. This is very apparent in community schools which have additional budgets so that they can make wider educational provision for the community. Members of the community perceive the school to be theirs and forge links. They also see the school at first hand and have the opportunity to view displays of children's work. Many headteachers have little difficulty in convincing people of the worth of their school once they have got them through the door; the problem is getting them through the door in the first place. Use of the school by external groups is a positive way of building links to achieve this. There are also some key groups such as pre-school playgroups, Brownies or Cubs – the next generation of potential pupils – whose members can come into the school. Both the general enhancement of the school's reputation by expanding community links and the more specific forging of relationships with potential new pupils are activities which the school should encourage. The balance has always to be kept between this use and the way that it complements or detracts from the main educational activity.

Displays in the school and in the locality

Inside the school one of the most positive images for visitors is displays of pupils' work. Schools that have long bare corridors not only create a dull environment but also miss a significant marketing opportunity. Outside the school, displaying pupils' work in local libraries, banks or building societies can be a good promotional approach. It can reinforce pupils' and staff's pride in their work and it can overcome some of the adverse publicity which the education system often receives.

Industry links

Building links with local commercial and industrial firms should be seen as a long-term activity. The benefits can be in terms of work experience places for pupils, job prospects for school leavers and sponsorship. The blanket approach of writing to a large number of firms is usually ineffective. What is needed is a more personal and targeted approach where links are built up over a period of time to achieve mutual benefits.

While we do not propose that this is an exhaustive list of the ways in which the school can promote itself it does illustrate the possibilities available if a co-ordinated approach is used to exploit the opportunities that present themselves.

Conclusion

This chapter has outlined a number of promotional techniques that are available. Schools should employ them to meet defined marketing needs and not as an end in themselves. It is too easy to be seduced into producing a new prospectus or writing press releases with glorious prose. With little time and few resources schools need to focus their activity to reap the maximum benefit from their efforts. To achieve this, the promotional techniques have to be part of the marketing strategy. The way in which they can be employed in this context will be considered in the next chapter.

References

Bradley, H. (1996) 'Parental choice of schools in an area containing grant-maintained schools', *School Organisation*, 16(1), pp 59–69.

Devlin, T. and Knight, B. (1990) *Public Relations and Marketing for Schools*, Harlow, Longman.

Exercise 10.1 People and marketing

List ways in which each of the following can be more effectively informed and how they can help publicise the school:

1 Pupils
2 Parents
3 Professionals
4 Public

Exercise 10.2 Design of prospectuses, brochures and flyers

Form a prospectus review group and undertake the following tasks:

1 Using the key points in prospectus design listed in this chapter, consider your school prospectus and find three or four exemplars of good practice.
2 In the same way, list three or four examples of how your prospectus could be improved to meet the key points.
3 Repeat the two process above (questions 1 and 2) for the school brochure and flyer.

Exercise 10.3 Distribution of prospectuses, brochures and flyers

Visit the locations listed below and check any school literature or information you find there.

	Material available	Quality of display/material on a scale of 1 to 5 (5 = excellent)
Nursery, primary or middle schools		
Public libraries		
Information centres		
Citizens' Advice Bureaux		
Estate agents and removal firms		
Doctors' and dentists' waiting rooms, clinics, hairdressers		
Local business firms		
Local press and media		

Exercise 10.4 Other written material

Form a task group of parents, governors, pupils and teachers to assemble and evaluate the material listed in the table below on a scale of 1 to 5 (5 = excellent) using the following criteria: a) high quality; b) first impression; c) use of corporate image; d) mistakes.

	High quality	**First impression**	**Use of corporate image**	**Mistakes**
Newsletter				
Headed paper				
Prospectus				
Curriculum information sheets				
Letters home				
Staff recruitment information				
Student reports/Records of Achievement				
Press advertising				

Exercise 10.5 Open evenings

Appoint a task group to evaluate open evenings on a five-point scale where 1 = poor and 5 = excellent. Assess the following by circling the appropriate number:

State of the entrance hall	1	2	3	4	5
Quality of initial reception by staff/students of the school	1	2	3	4	5
Students showing parents around	1	2	3	4	5
Quality of displays around the school	1	2	3	4	5
Willingness of staff to answer questions	1	2	3	4	5
Layout of the main hall	1	2	3	4	5
State of the main hall	1	2	3	4	5
Presentations – oral	1	2	3	4	5
Clarity of what was said	1	2	3	4	5
Presentation material – written	1	2	3	4	5
De-briefing of the staff the following morning	1	2	3	4	5
Aggregating the information received	1	2	3	4	5

11

Implementing the Marketing Plan

Go for gold

Introduction

This chapter is rather different in structure compared to the earlier ones. We suggest an appropriate process for building and implementing a marketing plan and, as we go through the plan, we provide exercises to help you to structure your own activity. We show how to integrate the concepts discussed earlier in the book with the time-sequenced operational plan. We put forward four key aspects which should help schools.

- The time sequence of the stages in the marketing process/plan.
- The role of the people involved.
- The key marketing actions/activities to be undertaken.
- The implementation of these actions/activities.

The time sequence of the marketing plan

In order to analyse good practice, we take as a case study example Brentwich School. In the past the school has involved itself in little coherent marketing, having previously engaged in a series of *ad hoc* responses to marketing issues, but it now wants to integrate marketing into its planning process. We divide the academic year into six time periods equivalent to the traditional school half terms, so that there are six periods prior to the launch of the marketing strategy the following September. If we count backwards through the time periods starting from the launch, we can refer to them as T–1, T–2, and so on. Fig 11.1 indicates how this can be shown.

Sept/Oct	Nov/Dec	Jan/Feb	Feb/Mar	April/May	Jun/Jul	Sept
T – 6 →	T – 5 →	T – 4 →	T – 3 →	T – 2 →	T – 1 →	T

Fig 11.1 Activity time periods

The activities which might take place in the time periods are as shown in Fig 11.2.

T – **6**	Create an awareness and an understanding of the importance of marketing in the school – training day using visiting speaker, followed by data on school enrolments, parent relationships, and discussion groups.
T – **5**	Build 'strategic intent' by focus groups, team-building exercises and articulating aims and mission of the school in consistent and regular way.
T – **4**	Conduct Marketing Analysis 1 – analyse the school using client attitude surveys (*see* Chapter Eight and Appendices).
T – **3**	Conduct Marketing Analysis 2 – carry out analysis of competitors, environment and client base (*see* Chapters Five, Six and Seven).
T – **2**	Interpret data gained in T – 4 and T – 3 through a SWOT, BCG or lifecycle analysis (*see* Chapter Nine) and formulate a marketing plan.
T – **1**	Produce marketing materials, brief participants, alert press, etc.
T	Launch and activate marketing strategy.

Fig 11.2 Time sequence of activities

The advantages of carefully analysing and working through a time plan like this can be seen in a number of ways.

- It integrates the internal and external markets by carefully starting from awareness and strategic intent and then moving on to analysis and implementation.
- In overcrowded and overloaded management schedules it adopts a staged and manageable approach. It avoids the 'instant response' in favour of a thought-out and planned campaign.
- It should aid the focusing of the marketing effort on a few key activities that the analysis has shown are likely to have the greatest impact.

The role of the people involved

Finding members for a marketing team

Now that those responsible for the overall management of the school's marketing plan have stated in broad terms what has to be done, it is necessary to involve a wider group of people in order to divide up the work. This group will be particularly helpful when it is time to prepare and disseminate promotional material. However, in order to have commitment to the strategies, it is wise to involve this wider group at an early stage, for example during strategic market analysis, so that they can translate the marketing aims into objectives. A team, rather than an individual approach will be needed. This is to avoid too much work falling on too few people and, if carefully managed, it also helps to ensure a coherent message and a co-ordinated effort. When deciding who to involve, it is important to remember the broader client groups which were described in Chapter One. Involvement in the development and implementation of the marketing strategy will reinforce the messages which the school is anxious to communicate. The next exercise looks at the aspects of finding a team but it must be emphasised that the various partners in the school should be consulted about their possible roles, rather than have assumptions made about their preferences.

Exercise 11.1 Finding a marketing team

1 Who is responsible for the overall marketing of your school?	
2 Who could help to develop and deploy the marketing strategy?	
Groups	**Possible contribution**
Governors (you may wish to name them or to subdivide by type)	
Staff • Teaching • Classroom support • Clerical • Technical • Caretaking • Cleaning • Lunchtime supervisors	
Regular visitors and helpers (it is helpful to list the various types)	
Current pupils (by year group)	
Parents	
Others, including the external clients (list types)	

Building a marketing team culture

Once the managers of the marketing process have decided who will help with the marketing strategy, then it is worth spending some time building that group of people into a team with a common culture. This will involve getting them together and ensuring that they all have a common view of the mission and aims of the school and that they all understand their role in developing and implementing the strategy which will communicate messages about the school to the wider group of clients. As we have discussed above, it is preferable if the team is involved at the earliest possible stages of the marketing process. The following list of features of a team, as opposed to an *ad hoc* group, should help the managers to focus on issues which must be addressed at this stage. A team:

- shares a common purpose
- plans the way in which it will operate
- uses the skills and knowledge of all its members
- recognises the contributions of all its members
- uses its time effectively
- works towards consensus
- has the full commitment of its members to any decisions
- makes decisions which can be implemented
- evaluates and improves the processes which it uses.

Exercise 11.2 will enable you to build a marketing team.

Exercise 11.2 Building the team and its culture

1 List the people in your marketing team.
2 When will the team first meet?
3 List the desired outcomes of that meeting. The following may provide a starting point: • Team members should know each other. • Team members should understand the aims of the marketing strategy. • Team members should have an understanding of the marketing activities carried out so far. • Team members should have a shared view of the team's role.
4 What sort of activities must take place at that meeting in order to achieve each of the desired outcomes?

The key marketing actions/activities to be undertaken

It is important to be clear about the aims and objectives of the marketing strategy and to determine priorities so that appropriate promotional approaches can be chosen for achievable outcomes.

Defining marketing aims

It is important to consider the *aims* to be achieved through the marketing strategy. Is the school trying to achieve a general increase in levels of awareness about its purpose or activities or is there a more specific aspect of its work which needs to be communicated to a particular client group? Aims tend to cover broad areas and are not usually achieved within a short timescale. There should be some recognition of this so that instant results are not expected. It is unlikely that aims will be achieved at all unless the various partners in the school have been involved in their development and understand the reasons for them. Both the process of formulating marketing aims and the communication of these aims are important steps in the development of the marketing strategy.

Exercise 11.3 Defining marketing aims

1 What are the aims of your marketing strategy?
2 How are the internal clients, in particular the staff, being made aware of these aims?
3 Do you have staff commitment to these aims?

Setting marketing objectives

Once the aims have been formulated and the team has been established, it is possible to move on to the setting of *objectives*. This should involve the team in taking an aim and agreeing the various objectives which must be met in order to achieve that aim. During this process each objective must be checked to ensure that it is specific, measurable, achievable, relevant and time-limited. Because of their specific nature, it is reasonable to develop objectives which will be achievable within one year. There will be ongoing monitoring and evaluation so that adjustments can be made or new objectives stated as time goes on.

Exercise 11.4 Setting marketing objectives

<table>
<tr><td colspan="2">

1. Write one of your marketing aims here.

....

Now list the short term steps to achieving this aim. These can then be adjusted so that they are expressed as objectives.

</td></tr>
<tr><td colspan="2">

2. For each of the steps listed above, work through the following process.

</td></tr>
<tr><td>State the objective</td><td>Is it:
• written?
• clear?
• specific?</td></tr>
<tr><td>How will you know when it has been achieved?</td><td>Is it:
• measurable:
– quantitatively?
– qualitatively?</td></tr>
<tr><td>When should it be achieved?</td><td>Is it:
• timed?</td></tr>
<tr><td>Have you consulted those involved?</td><td>Is it:
• agreed?
• useful?
• relevant?
• achievable?
• challenging?</td></tr>
<tr><td>Do any objectives conflict?</td><td>If so, which?</td></tr>
<tr><td>What are the constraints?</td><td>Are resources available?
What are the pressures:
• internal?
• external?</td></tr>
<tr><td>Reassess</td><td>Is the objective still realistic?
If not, repeat process</td></tr>
</table>

Prioritising marketing objectives

If the process described in Exercise 11.4 is followed for each aim, then it is likely that there will be a very long list of objectives which may appear daunting. The school should place these into some kind of order which will relate partly to priorities and partly to a natural grouping of activities. It is very important that the school should focus on three or four major activities – for example a new prospectus, improved relations with the press and enhanced home–school links. This is because it is better to achieve this smaller number of objectives rather than having an extensive list which, through of pressure of work, would not be completed. The school year is quite clearly divided into terms so this may prove a good starting point for the grouping and prioritising of the objectives. Exercise 11.5 asks you to state the objectives for the whole year and then to focus down in order to establish priorities.

Exercise 11.5 Prioritising marketing objectives

1 What are your objectives for this *year*? List them and then mark them as A, B or C according to the urgency with which they must be achieved.

2 What are your objectives for this *term*? You will probably list all the category As from above but should also check whether any of the Bs must be achieved within this short timescale.

Add to this list any objectives which should, for reasons of logistics, rather than urgency, be achieved during this term.

If you have included many Bs in this coming term, it may be that you are being over-optimistic about what can be achieved.

3 What are your objectives for this *month*? Mark against each the date by which it should be achieved.

Choosing the promotional approaches

The team will now have to devise a strategy for achieving the objectives within the planned timescale. Part of the role of the team should be to consider the promotional approaches which were described in Chapter Ten alongside the marketing objectives and to draw up a resource bid to senior management which will allow the marketing aims to be realised.

Exercise 11.6 Choosing the promotional approaches

1	**Write down an objective or a group of linked objectives.** **Who is/are the target group(s) in this case?**
2	**Which promotional approaches are likely to offer the most effective means of achieving the objective(s)?**
3	**Which resources are likely to be needed and what are they likely to cost in terms of materials, postage, labour?**
4	**Indicate any resources which are available at no cost, or any income which is likely to be generated if these approaches are used, for example voluntary help and advertising revenue.**
5	**Summarise on one side of A4 the objectives to be achieved, the timescale, the preferred strategies and the resources which are required. It is essential to include the cost of the school staff, such as the office staff or technicians, as they represent a real cost to the school.**

The implementation of the marketing activities

Five questions are significant here.

1. What activity is to be undertaken?
2. What resources are needed to facilitate the activity?
3. Who is responsible for undertaking the activity and is accountable for it?
4. In which time period will the activity take place?
5. What performance measures will be used to evaluate the success of the marketing activity?

You may wish to copy Fig 11.3 to aid your planning.

Activity	
Resources/materials required	
Individual responsible	
Time period	
Performance measures	

Fig 11.3 Action grid

Conclusion

This chapter has described how a marketing strategy can be planned for implementation. It is important that the plans are realistic and focused. Achieving a limited number of objectives and building on them the following year is better than having a large number of half completed objectives. Marketing is a process that is ongoing and schools should not attempt too much in a rush of initial enthusiasm at the expense of a properly paced marketing strategy which will build up over a number of years.

12

■ ■ ■

Evaluating the Marketing Process

'Can you tell me how we did?'

If a school is expending time and effort on marketing, then it must ensure that the marketing effort is focused and, above all, is producing results. Just as a school evaluates its educational product to ensure that the educational aims and objectives which it sets itself have been met, it must also assess how far the aims and objectives of the marketing strategy have been achieved.

The monitoring process should be targeted so that specific information can be obtained about how effective a particular marketing strategy or activity has been. If a more general attempt is made to evaluate the whole marketing process then it will be impossible to attribute the success to different elements and difficult to know which approaches to prioritise for maximum effect in the following year.

Once the marketing strategy has been developed, two types of monitoring take place: the monitoring of the implementation process and the monitoring of the impact of the strategy. The first of these two monitoring processes is to check on the 'action' element. Has the named person produced the necessary material or made the specified contacts or has the draft material come back from the printers? These are the sort of ongoing checking and monitoring activities that were suggested in Chapter Eleven and which need to precede an assessment of the effectiveness of the marketing strategy.

Many of the approaches and techniques outlined in the chapter on market research (Chapter Four) can be employed to assess the effectiveness of the marketing strategy. We use the example of Brentwich School once more to illustrate how these techniques can be applied.

Brentwich School, over a two- or three-year period, decided to target a number of marketing activities in order to improve aspects of the school's relationship with its clients. These included:

1 The improvement of the open day/evening attendance through the use of better publicity to attract more prospective parents and pupils to the event.
2 The production of a new, higher quality prospectus for promotional purposes.
3 The development of better quality advertisements and job specification material for new staff in order to attract suitable recruits.
4 The improvement of home–school communications.

How can the school monitor and evaluate the effectiveness of its marketing effort in these areas? It is first necessary to assume that the management structures and approaches outlined in Chapter Eleven have been put into place and that the individual items form part of a coherent marketing strategy. Three basic questions have to be asked:

- What did the school plan to do?
- What did the school actually do?
- What was the effect of this action?

The first two questions define the precise scope and implementation of the strategy. If an element of the strategy is missing then the effect of the marketing may be distorted and it is necessary to assess whether the overall strategy was ineffective or whether it was the process of implementation that was at fault. When these two questions have been answered, the most important one – that of assessing the effect of the marketing strategy – can be answered. To illustrate the type of measures that can be used to assess the effect of a strategy, each of the Brentwich School marketing activities will be analysed in turn.

1 *The improvement of the open day/evening attendance through the use of better publicity to attract more prospective parents and pupils to the event.* The easiest way to assess the success of this activity is to count the number of people who came! Obvious as it sounds, many schools make generalisations about the number of people who attend and there is no specific attempt to calculate how many people came through the door. Similarly, it is important to find out where the people came from. Were they from an area where the school had targeted advertising so that it could be assumed that they had come in response to that? Or did they come from a different area for different reasons? Staff involved in the event should be asked to enquire about these factors. Similarly, staff should ask about what had attracted prospective parents to the school and what they found valuable about the information they received at the open day. This sort of enquiry can be followed up through postal questionnaires to people who attended (if their addresses have been kept) or by personal communication when children are enrolled at the school. However, it may be that the parents who do not

choose the school provide the more valuable information. In the long term, the most important form of assessment is, of course, whether more pupils attend the school as a result of this type of activity.

2 *The production of a new, higher quality prospectus for promotional purposes.* It is quite easy to collect data on the number of requests for further details about the school or for visits to the school. However, it is difficult to demonstrate a direct correlation between a new prospectus and any rise in such figures. Nevertheless, such data can help to feed into a wider information system regarding the value of the new prospectus. Office staff can be briefed to try, when they receive telephone calls, to gauge people's attitudes to the documentation which has been sent to them. New parents can be asked if the information is helpful and if the presentation is attractive, creating a positive response to the school and smoothing the transfer process for their children. Evidence can also be collected from staff as to whether the prospectus creates a positive image and pride in the school.

3 *The development of better quality advertisements and job specification material for new staff in order to attract suitable recruits.* The effectiveness of this could be assessed by comparing previous performance with the current position in a number of areas: the number of requests received for information and application forms; the number of application forms submitted; the quality of applicants and subsequent interviewees; and, above all, the number of posts subsequently filled with appropriate staff. This type of information provides very useful evidence of the success of the marketing effort in this area.

4 *The improvement of home–school communications.* A very good example of this was provided in Chapter Eight which looked at the use of questionnaires. Similarly, a random selection of parents can be telephoned on a regular basis to seek opinions on the type and quality of information being received. Quantitative assessment of the number of parents attending events, returning reply slips or commenting on reports can indicate the successful transmission of information and involvement.

Conclusion

All these suggestions indicate ways in which the school can assess whether the marketing activities have been successful. It would be wrong to assume that evaluation is easy or that a perfect correlation between effort and result can be achieved. This should not prevent significant indicators being used as a guide for future action as long as they are interpreted in context and with sensitivity. Thus, evaluation is essential if the time, effort and resources allocated to marketing are to be well spent and to yield results. Schools must design their evaluation indicators to make an assessment which will guide the marketing strategy so as to maximise the results from their efforts.

Exercise 12.1 Monitoring and evaluation

1 List the marketing activities which were planned for your school for the term/year.

2 Which were completed?

How was progress monitored?

What factors contributed to their completion according to plan?

3 Which were not completed?

Why were they not completed?

How can the situation be rectified?

Exercise 12.2 Evaluation of the impact of a marketing activity

This exercise should be completed at the *planning* stage, not when an activity is complete.

1 Which marketing activity is to be evaluated?
2 When will the activity be completed? **When will the evaluation take place?** **Who will carry out the evaluation?**
3 How will the evaluation be carried out? **What success indicators can be established for the marketing activity?**

Appendix 1

■ ■ ■

Categorised Questions

Student Survey 1997

Category	Questions	
Teaching and learning	1	In school, do you spend about the right amount of time on basic skills (such as reading, writing, mathematics)?
	4	Are you set the right type of homework?
	11	Are you set the right amount of homework?
	15	Are you satisfied with the way that your work is assessed?
	18	Are you happy with the size of your classes (i.e. the number of students in them)?
	23	Are you happy with the way that your achievement is recognised?
	9	Are you set challenging work that stretches you?
Satisfaction with staff	17	Are you satisfied with your Headteacher?
	22	Are you satisfied with your Deputy Headteacher(s)?
	2	Are you satisfied with the support staff (secretaries, caretaker, technicians, etc.)?
	26	On the whole, are you satisfied with your teachers?
	10	On the whole, do you feel that your teachers are interested in you?
	19	Are you satisfied with the help given by your teachers when you don't understand the work?
Communications	3	Are you satisfied with what the school tells your parents about how you are doing at school?
	27	Are you satisfied with the say that you have in school decisions that affect you?

Behaviour	6	Are you satisfied with the behaviour of other students *in* class?
	12	Are you satisfied with the behaviour of other students *out of* class?
	16	Are you satisfied with the school rules (code of conduct)?
	24	Are you satisfied with the way that other students treat you?
	30	Are you satisfied that the rules on attendance are applied fairly?
Facilities	5	Are you satisfied with lunch arrangements in the school?
	20	Are you satisfied with the extra-curricular activities (sports, concerts, clubs, etc.)?
	25	Are you satisfied with the school buildings, grounds and equipment?
	13	Are you satisfied with the services of the school library?
	28	Are you satisfied with the cleanliness of your school?
General	21	Are you satisfied with your school in general?
	7	Would you recommend a friend to come to this school?
Equal opportunities	29	Do you think that you get the same opportunities to do things as other people in your class?
	14	On the whole, do your teachers treat you fairly?
	8	Do you consider that your views are valued by the staff of the school?

What single change would improve your educational experience and enjoyment within the school?

Please use this box to make any further comments.

Parent Survey 1997

Category		Questions
Teaching and learning	1	Do you feel that the school is offering the right type of education for your child?
	4	Do you feel that your child is sufficiently challenged by the school to encourage maximum learning and development?
	11	Do you feel that the number of students in your child's classes is appropriate?
	18	Do you feel that your child is set the right type of homework?
	15	Do you feel that your child is set the right amount of homework?
Satisfaction with staff	23	In general, are you satisfied with your child's form teacher?
	17	In general, are you satisfied with your child's subject teachers?
	9	In general, are you satisfied with the Headteacher?
	22	In general, are you satisfied with the Deputy Headteacher(s)?
	2	Do you feel that the support staff at the school, such as secretaries, caretaker, catering staff, are helpful and friendly?
Communications	10	Are you satisfied with the information provided by the school about what your child is expected to learn?
	26	Are you satisfied with the information provided by the school about how your child is expected to behave?
	19	Do you feel you have an opportunity to discuss issues that affect your child?
	3	Do you feel you are being satisfactorily informed about your child's learning progress?
	27	Are you satisfied with your involvement in your child's school?

Discipline/Pastoral	6	Do you feel student discipline is being handled fairly at the school?
	12	Are you satisfied with the way that your child is looked after and supported in the school?
	16	Are you satisfied with the way that attendance is being monitored at the school?
Facilities	24	Are you satisfied with the extra-curricular programmes at the school (sports, concerts, clubs, etc.)?
	30	Are you satisfied with the library services at your child's school?
	5	Are you satisfied with the cleanliness of your child's school?
	20	Are you satisfied with the lunch-time arrangements?
Satisfaction/ Quality	25	Do you feel that your child likes the school?
	13	Do you feel welcome at the school?
	28	Generally, are you satisfied with your child's school?
	21	Would you recommend the school to new parents moving into the area?
Governors	7	Do you understand the role of the governors?
	29	In general, are you satisfied with the governing body?
	14	Do you feel that you receive adequate communication from the governors?
	8	Do you feel that there are adequate opportunities to represent your views to the governors?

What change, if any, would improve your child's education at the school?

Please expand on any question or make any further comments if you wish.

Teaching Staff Survey 1997

Please answer the following questionnaire within the context of schools in the 1990s:

Category	Questions	
Communications	1	Do you feel that there is good communication in your school?
	4	Do you feel that sufficient information is provided by your department *to the students* about what they are expected *to learn*?
	11	Do you feel that sufficient information is provided by your department *to parents* about what their children are expected *to learn*?
	15	Do you feel that sufficient information is provided by the school *to the students* about how they are expected *to behave*?
	18	Do you feel that sufficient information is provided by the school *to parents* about how their children are expected *to behave*?
Working environment	23	Are the facilities in the staff room satisfactory?
	9	Are you generally satisfied with the equipment and materials available to you for teaching?
	17	Are you generally satisfied with the quality of your teaching rooms?
	22	Do you feel that the number of students in the classes that you teach is appropriate?
	2	Are you satisfied with the school library?

Professional environment	26	Do you feel your assigned work responsibilities are fair and reasonable?
	10	Are you satisfied with your involvement in the decision-making process?
	19	Do you feel that the workload in your department is distributed equitably?
	3	Do you feel that you have adequate opportunities for professional development?
	27	Do you get adequate recognition and appreciation (from your colleagues) for your performance and accomplishments?
Quality of education	6	Do you feel that the school is providing a high quality education for its students?
	12	Would you recommend that a friend should send his/her child to the school?
	16	Would you recommend a colleague to work here?
	24	Do you feel that your school is a good place to work?
	30	Given the nature of the intake, do you think that there is a good level of student achievement in the school?
	5	Do you believe that the pastoral system adequately supports the students so that they can get the most out of their education?
Professional support	20	Do you feel you get support when you need it from the Headteacher?
	25	Do you feel you get support when you need it from the Deputy Headteacher(s)?
	13	Do you feel you get support when you need it from your colleagues?
	28	Are you satisfied with the *parental* involvement in educational activities and programmes provided at your school?
	21	Are you satisfied with the involvement of the *non-parent* community in educational activities and programmes at your school?

Governors	7	In general, are you satisfied with the governing body?
	29	Do you feel that you receive adequate communication from the governors?
	14	Do you feel that there are adequate opportunities to represent your views to the governors?
General	8	Do you find teaching at the school to be more rewarding than last year?

Please expand on any question or make any further comments if you wish.

Appendix 2

■ ■ ■

Randomised Questionnaires

Student Survey 1997

Boy/Girl

Year: ____________________ **Form:** __________________

		Yes	No	Not sure
1	In school do you spend about the right amount of time on basic skills (such as reading, writing, mathematics)?			
2	Are you satisfied with the support staff (secretaries, caretaker, technicians, etc.)?			
3	Are you satisfied with what the school tells your parents about how you are doing at school?			
4	Are you set the right type of homework?			
5	Are you satisfied with lunch arrangements in the school?			
6	Are you satisfied with the behaviour of other students *in* class?			
7	Would you recommend a friend to come to this school?			
8	Do you consider that your views are valued by the staff of the school?			
9	Are you set challenging work that stretches you?			
10	On the whole, do you feel that your teachers are interested in you?			
11	Are you set the right amount of homework?			
12	Are you satisfied with the behaviour of other students *out of* class?			
13	Are you satisfied with the services of the school library?			
14	On the whole, do your teachers treat you fairly?			
15	Are you satisfied with the way that your work is assessed?			

		Yes	No	Not sure
16	Are you satisfied with the school rules (code of conduct)?			
17	Are you satisfied with your Headteacher?			
18	Are you happy with the size of your classes (i.e. the number of students in them)?			
19	Are you satisfied with the help given by your teachers when you don't understand the work?			
20	Are you satisfied with the extra-curricular activities (sports, concerts, clubs, etc.)?			
21	Are you satisfied with your school in general?			
22	Are you satisfied with your Deputy Headteacher(s)?			
23	Are you happy with the way that your achievement is recognised?			
24	Are you satisfied with the way that other students treat you?			
25	Are you satisfied with the school buildings, grounds and equipment?			
26	On the whole, are you satisfied with your teachers?			
27	Are you satisfied with the say that you have in school decisions that affect you?			
28	Are you satisfied with the cleanliness of your school?			
29	Do you think that you get the same opportunities to do things as other people in your class?			
30	Are you satisfied that the rules on attendance are applied fairly?			

What single change would improve your educational experience and enjoyment within the school?

Please use this box to make any further comments.

Parent Survey 1997

Boy/Girl

Year: ____________________ **Form:** __________________

		Yes	**No**	**Not sure**
1	Do you feel that the school is offering the right type of education for your child?			
2	Do you feel that the support staff at the school, such as secretaries, caretaker, catering staff, are helpful and friendly?			
3	Do you feel you are being satisfactorily informed about your child's learning progress?			
4	Do you feel that your child is sufficiently challenged by the school to encourage maximum learning and development?			
5	Are you satisfied with the cleanliness of your child's school?			
6	Do you feel that student discipline is being handled fairly at the school?			
7	Do you understand the role of the governors?			
8	Do you feel that there are adequate opportunities to represent your views to the governors?			
9	In general are you satisfied with the Headteacher?			
10	Are you satisfied with the information provided by the school about what your child is expected to learn?			
11	Do you feel that the number of students in your child's classes is appropriate?			
12	Are you satisfied with the way that your child is looked after and supported in the school?			
13	Do you feel welcome at the school?			

		Yes	No	Not sure
14	Do you feel that you receive adequate communication from the governors?			
15	Do you feel that your child is set the right amount of homework?			
16	Are you satisfied with the way that attendance is being monitored at the school?			
17	In general, are you satisfied with your child's subject teachers?			
18	Do you feel that your child is set the right type of homework?			
19	Do you feel you have an opportunity to discuss issues that affect your child?			
20	Are you satisfied with the lunch-time arrangements?			
21	Would you recommend the school to new parents moving into the area?			
22	In general, are you satisfied with your Deputy Headteacher(s)?			
23	In general, are you satisfied with your child's form teacher?			
24	Are you satisfied with the extra-curricular programmes at the school (sports, concerts, clubs etc.)?			
25	Do you feel that your child likes the school?			
26	Are you satisfied with the information provided by the school about how your child is expected to behave?			
27	Are you satisfied with your involvement in your child's school?			
28	Generally, are you satisfied with your child's school?			
29	In general, are you satisfied with the governing body?			
30	Are you satisfied with the library services at your child's school?			

What change, if any, would improve your child's education at the school?

Please expand on any question or make any further comments if you wish.

Teaching Staff Survey 1997

Please answer the following questionnaire within the context of schools in the 1990s.

		Yes	**No**	**Not sure**
1	Do you feel that there is good communication in your school?			
2	Are you satisfied with the school library?			
3	Do you feel that you have adequate opportunities for professional development?			
4	Do you feel that sufficient information is provided by your department *to the students* about what they are expected *to learn*?			
5	Do you believe that the pastoral system adequately supports the students so that they can get the most out of their education?			
6	Do you feel that the school is providing a high quality education for its students?			
7	In general, are you satisfied with the governing body?			
8	Do you find teaching at the school to be more rewarding than last year?			
9	Are you generally satisfied with the equipment and materials available to you for teaching?			
10	Are you satisfied with your involvement in the decision-making process?			
11	Do you feel that sufficient information is provided by your department *to parents* about what their children are expected *to learn*?			
12	Would you recommend that a friend should send his/her child to the school?			
13	Do you feel that you get support when you need it from your colleagues?			
14	Do you feel that there are adequate opportunities to represent your views to the governors?			

		Yes	No	Not sure
15	Do you feel that sufficient information is provided by the school *to the students* about how they are expected *to behave*?			
16	Would you recommend a colleague to work here?			
17	Are you generally satisfied with the quality of your teaching rooms?			
18	Do you feel that sufficient information is provided by the school *to parents* about how their children are expected *to behave*?			
19	Do you feel that the workload in your department is distributed equitably?			
20	Do you feel that you get support when you need it from the Headteacher?			
21	Are you satisfied with the involvement of the *non-parent* community in educational activities and programmes at your school?			
22	Do you feel that the number of students in the classes that you teach is appropriate?			
23	Are the facilities in the staff room satisfactory?			
24	Do you feel that your school is a good place to work?			
25	Do you feel that you get support when you need it from the Deputy Headteacher(s)?			
26	Do you feel that your assigned work responsibilities are fair and reasonable?			
27	Do you get adequate recognition and appreciation from your colleagues for your performance and accomplishments?			
28	Are you satisfied with the *parental* involvement in educational activities and programmes provided at your school?			
29	Do you feel that you receive adequate communication from the governors?			
30	Given the nature of the intake, do you think that there is a good level of student achievement in the school?			

Please expand on any question or make any further comments if you wish.

Staff Survey 1997

Please answer the following questionnaire within the context of schools in the 1990s.

		Yes	No	Not sure
1	Do you feel that there is good communication in your school?			
2	Are you satisfied with the facilities at break for children?			
3	Do you feel that you have adequate opportunities for professional development?			
4	Do you feel that sufficient information is provided by teachers *to the pupils* about what they are expected *to learn*?			
5	Do you believe that the pastoral system adequately supports the children so that they can get the most out of their education?			
6	Do you feel that the school is providing a high quality education for its pupils?			
7	In general, are you satisfied with the governing body?			
8	Do you find working at the school to be more rewarding than last year?			
9	Are you generally satisfied with the equipment and materials available to you to carry out your jobs?			
10	Are you satisfied with your involvement in the decision-making process?			
11	Do you feel that sufficient information is provided by the school *to parents* about what their children are expected *to learn*?			
12	Would you recommend that a friend should send his/her child to the school?			
13	Do you feel that you get support when you need it from your colleagues?			
14	Do you feel that there are adequate opportunities to represent your views to the governors?			

		Yes	No	Not sure
15	Do you feel that sufficient information is provided by the school *to the pupils* about how they are expected *to behave*?			
16	Would you recommend a colleague to work here?			
17	Are you generally satisfied with the quality of the rooms in which you work?			
18	Do you feel that sufficient information is provided by the school *to parents* about how their children are expected *to behave*?			
19	Do you feel that the workload is distributed equitably between you and your colleagues?			
20	Do you feel that you get support when you need it from the Headteacher?			
21	Are you satisfied with the involvement of the *non-parent* community in educational activities and programmes at your school?			
22	Do you feel that the number of children in the classes is appropriate?			
23	Are the facilities in the staff room satisfactory?			
24	Do you feel that your school is a good place to work?			
25	Do you feel that you get support when you need it from the Deputy Headteacher(s)?			
26	Do you feel that your assigned work responsibilities are fair and reasonable?			
27	Do you get adequate recognition and appreciation from your colleagues for your performance and accomplishments?			
28	Are you satisfied with the *parental* involvement in educational activities and programmes provided at your school?			
29	Do you feel that you receive adequate communication from the governors?			
30	Given the nature of the intake, do you think that there is a good level of pupil achievement in the school?			

Please expand on any question or make any further comments if you wish.

Appendix 3

■ ■ ■

Investigating the attitudes of Years 1 and 2 at Buswells Lodge Primary School

'Ask the Clients' Survey 1996/7

The following background to the survey was supplied by Michel Riley, the headteacher of Buswells Lodge Primary School.

The survey was trialled in 1995/6 with two Year 6 and two Year 5 classes. The headteacher had slightly amended some of the questions to provide a more 'primary-friendly' style of language. For instance, the terms 'pupils' and 'children' were substituted in place of 'students'. The survey material was explained to staff and governors and the original responses were gained with the headteacher alone assisting pupils to complete the survey questionnaires. Great care was taken to ensure that no guidance was given which might have affected the responses and that there was standardisation in the presentation of the material.

Following this initial year, a group of teachers and ancillary staff met to consider extending the survey to all year groups in the school. It was felt that there were still problems associated with the style of some of the questions and the group spent some time considering a preferred form of words which still allowed the responses to be grouped in the manner of the original survey.

It was agreed that class teachers and ancillary staff would work with the youngest children (Years 1 and 2) in a group setting to complete the questionnaire. A brief training session was held and through discussion staff raised their awareness of the risk of 'leading' responses and the potential for creating collective agreement in groups of responders. It was felt that help could be given to children who might wish to express an opinion on the service provided by an individual known to them by name (for example, Mr Riley), but not by job title (Headteacher).

It was recognised that there was a potential for children 'spoiling' their papers by responding in all three categories (Yes, No, Not sure), but it was agreed that such responses would not be rejected by the adult group, but that the attention of the child would be drawn to the problem. If the child repeated the 'error', it would not be further commented upon. Free text responses were checked by the adult and, if necessary, correct spellings were recorded on the child's behalf, using their own words. Drawings were annotated by the adult from discussion with the child. Where children sought affirmation of the 'correctness' of their answer, this would be gently deflected, but support would be voiced for the answer the child seemed to prefer. Copying by one child of another's response would be notified to the copier, but no further action would be taken.

Buswells Lodge Primary School
Pupil Survey 1996

Are you a boy? ☐ ✓ or x Are you a girl? ☐ ✓ or x

Year group .... Class teacher ....

		Yes	No	Not sure
1	In school do you think you spend about the right amount of time doing reading, writing, mathematics (basic skills)?			
2	Are you happy with the help you and the school get from adults other than your teacher (secretaries, caretaker, ancillaries)?			
3	Are you satisfied with what the school tells your parents about how you are doing at school?			
4	Are you set the right type of homework?			
5	Are you satisfied with lunch arrangements in the school?			
6	Are you happy with the behaviour of other children in your class?			
7	Is this a good school for your friends to come to?			
8	Do you think that your views and thoughts about the school are seen as important by the staff?			
9	Is the work you do hard enough?			
10	On the whole, do you feel that your teachers are interested in you?			
11	Are you set the right amount of homework?			
12	Are you happy with the behaviour of other children out of class?			
13	Do you think the school library is good?			
14	On the whole, are the teachers fair to you?			
15	Are you happy with the way your work is marked and commented upon?			

		Yes	No	Not sure
16	Are you happy with the school rules (code of conduct)?			
17	Are you happy with your Headteacher?			
18	Are you happy with the size of your classes (i.e. the number of pupils in them)?			
19	Are you happy with the help your teacher gives you when you don't understand the work?			
20	Are you happy with the after-school activities (sports, concerts, clubs etc.)?			
21	Are you satisfied with your school in general?			
22	Are you happy with your Deputy Headteacher?			
23	Are you happy with the way that your achievement is recognised?			
24	Are you happy with way that other children treat you?			
25	Are you happy with the school buildings (classrooms, halls, mobiles), grounds, (playgrounds, field) and equipment?			
26	Usually are you satisfied with your teachers?			
27	Are you happy with the say that you have in school decisions that affect you?			
28	Are you happy with the cleanliness of your school?			
29	Do you think that you get the same chance to do things as other children in your class?			
30	Are you happy that the rules on attendance are applied fairly?			

What single change would improve your educational experience and enjoyment within the school?

Please use this box to make any further comments.

Thank you for completing this questionnaire.

Index

■ ■ ■

Abbott, R. 108, 112
Aburdene, P. 51, 55
advertising 165
Asch, D. 58, 60, 66

Bagley, C. 85, 86, 89
Bennis, W. 30, 38
Birchenhough, M. 108, 112
Boisot, M. 16, 17, 26
Boston Consulting Group matrix (BCG) 118, 124–7
Bowman, C. 58, 60, 66
Bradley, H. 86, 88, 89, 99
Brain, J. 86, 89
brochures 145–56, 177–8
Broughton Junior School 156–7
business strength 128–30
Buswells Lodge Primary School 223–7

Cain, J. 168, 171–2
Caldwell, B. J. 51, 55
cash cows 124, 126–7
Chaplain, R. 113
client 7, 8, 11–12, 31–7, 76–98
  attitude survey 108–11, 199–227
  behaviour 87–8
  needs 86–7
  satisfaction 100
  wants 85–6
client–focused culture 19, 29, 31–7
communication 4
competitive forces 58, 67
competitors 57–75
  existing 58–61
consumers 7
corporate identity 156
cost relationships 6
Crego, E. T. 37, 38
customers 7

Davies, B. 3, 14, 25, 26, 46, 51, 55, 109, 113, 137, 139
DES 5, 15
Devlin, T. 161, 175
DfEE 145
DION 108

dogs 124, 126–7

Education Reform Act 1988 5
Elliott-Kemp, J. 108, 113
Ellison, L. 3, 14, 25, 26, 46, 55, 109, 113, 137, 139
entrance hall 173
entrants, new 61
environment
  global 51
  local 53–4
  national 53
evaluation 193–7
  instruments 108

flyers 145–56, 177–8
focus groups 100, 111–12
formula-based funding 6
formula funding 5, 22
Fullan, M. 30, 38

Garratt, B. 16, 26
General Electric Screen 128–31
Glatter, R. 85, 86, 89
global
  environment 51
  trends 51–2
governors 8
GRIDS 108
group promotion 168, 169–70

Handy, C. 51, 55
Hounslow Manor School 154–5

Ilkley Pyramid of schools 168–70
image 100
industry links 175
information
  needs, identifying 44
  primary 46–7
  qualitiative 70–1
  quantitative 68–9
  secondary 45
interviews 100, 111–12

Jenkins, H. 30, 38

Kawasaki, G. 19, 26, 29, 30, 38, 137, 149
Kawasaki's matrix 118, 137–9
Klein, R. 86, 89
Knight, B. 161, 175

LEA 8
league tables 100, 108
Levačić, R. 14, 15
Little, A. D. 131, 139
Little's Lifecycle Analysis 118, 131–6

Macbeath, A. 109, 113
market
  attractiveness 128–9
  research 20, 41–9
    planning of 45
    steps in 43
    when 42–3
    who 43
    why 42
  segmentation 8
  segments 77–8
marketing
  aims 186–7
  evidence (interpreting and integrating) 118–39
  implementation 18, 19, 21
  mix 20–3
  objectives 188–9
  plan (implementation) 181–92
  plan (time sequence) 181–2)
  process (components of) 18–20
  process (context of) 20
  process (evaluation of) 193–7
  team 183–6
  techniques and approaches 143–80
markets
  as allocation systems 13
  external 8, 79–84
  internal 8, 77–8
media 160
monitoring 193–4, 196
myths and misconceptions 9–13

Naisbitt, J. 51, 55
name, school 168, 171–2
Nanus, B. 30, 38
needs 11–12, 86–7, 97
newsletters 158
newspapers 161, 164–5

OFSTED 8, 108
open
  day 166, 180
  enrolment 5
  evening 166, 180
opportunities 104, 107
option booklets 159

parent response 110
PASCI study 109, 113
people 23, 144–5
PEST analysis 56
place 23
Porter, M. 58, 66
positioning 23
price 22
proactive staff 19, 29, 37–8
problem child 124, 126–7
product 20
  benefits 21–2
  life 22
  quality 22
  range 21
products, replacement 63–4
promotion 23
promotional approaches 190
prospectuses 145–56, 177–8
providers, existing 58–61, 68

questionnaires 100, 108–11, 199–227

radio 161, 165
records of achievement 159
Reigate School 168, 171–2
relationships 4
report
  school 159
  annual to parents 160
research
  observation 47
  survey 47
Ruddock, J. 109, 113

Schiffrin, P. D. 37, 38
school reports 159
signs, school 173
Social Trends 53, 55
star 124, 126–7
Steadman, S. 108, 112
strategic
  cause 19, 29–31
  intent 16, 18 , 29
  market analysis 18, 19, 20
  planning 17
  thought 16
strengths 103–4, 105–7
suppliers 64–5

Surfside Primary School 152–3
SWOT 100, 101, 107, 118–23

Teacher Training Agency (TTA) 8
Technology Foresight 51, 55
telephone 108
television 160–1
threats 105, 107

uniform 172
users 65–6

video 167

Wallace, G. 113
wants 11–12, 85–6
weaknesses 104, 107
Weaver County Primary School
162–3
West, A. 85, 89
Williams, G. L. 108, 113
Woods, P. 85, 86, 89